W9-ACH-169

THE GLOBAL HISTORY SERIES

Leften Stavrianos, *Northwestern University*
General Editor

This series aims to present history in global perspective, going beyond national or regional limitations, and dealing with overriding trends and forces. The various collections of original materials span the globe, range from prehistoric times to the present, and include anthropology, economics, political science, and religion, as well as history.

Dr. Roland Oliver, co-editor of this volume, is one of Europe's leading experts on African history. Both a scholar and an adventurer, he has traveled extensively in Africa south of the Sahara and is the author of *The Missionary Factor in East Africa* and *The Dawn of African History*, and co-author of *A Short History of Africa* and the *Oxford History of East Africa*. Dr. Oliver, who is Professor of the History of Africa at the University of London, is also the co-founder and editor of The Journal of African History.

Caroline Oliver has accompanied her husband on his wide-ranging travels in Africa. An expert in her own right, she is the author of numerous articles on Africa which have appeared in the English press.

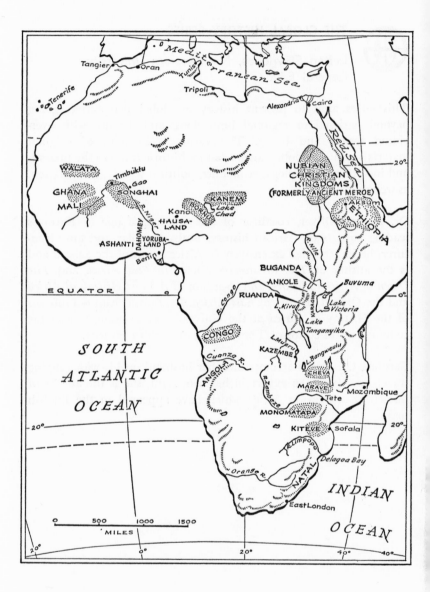

DT 7
O4

AFRICA IN THE DAYS
OF EXPLORATION

EDITED BY ROLAND OLIVER
AND CAROLINE OLIVER

AUG 5 1970

153102

A SPECTRUM BOOK   Prentice-Hall, Inc. / *Englewood Cliffs, N.J.*

Current printing (last digit):
11 10 9 8 7 6 5 4 3 2

Copyright © 1965 by Prentice-Hall, Inc. / *Englewood Cliffs, N.J.*
A SPECTRUM BOOK

All rights reserved. No part of this book may be reproduced in any form, by mimeograph or any other means, without permission in writing from the publishers.

Library of Congress Catalog Card No.: 65-23297
Printed in the United States of America—C

P01842
C01843

CONTENTS

AFRICA IN THE DAYS

OF EXPLORATION

Author's note

Almost all the texts in Part II refer to African countries where one or another of the many languages of the Bantu language family are spoken. These are highly inflected languages. The gender is expressed by prefixes which differ between one language and another. For the sake of simplicity the most usual set of prefixes has been used wherever these prefixes occur, irrespective of those used by the author of the extract. Thus "Bu" always denotes the country, "Lu" or "Ki" the language, "Mu" a person, male or female, of that country, and "Ba" persons, male or female. For example, Buganda, Luganda, Muganda, and Baganda refer respectively to the country, language, and people, singular and plural.

INTRODUCTION

In this book are collected descriptions of Negro Africa prior to the opening of the continent to European influences. They have been gathered in order to provide some background of primary materials against which the growing body of secondary historical works on Africa may be seen.

Negro Africa has been taken to mean every part of Africa where the population is of predominantly Negro, or of mixed Negro origin. In so vast an area, constituting more than three quarters of the third largest continent, it has been impossible to effect any over-all historical arrangement. As far as possible, pieces have been grouped in chronological order within an area, or within a state or group of states. This arrangement, naturally, has been easier to achieve with pieces concerning West Africa, where the source material outweighs all the rest.

The chronological range of works presented is very wide, stretching from the Muslim travelers and geographers of the tenth century to the European explorers of the nineteenth. This range in time is dictated by the availability of the best material. Some indigenous material, consisting of oral tradition, both prose and poetry, which has been recorded since literacy reached Africa, is also included to provide some indication of what the unwritten literature of Africa was like.

Although the geographical canvas is immense, and although the writers who sketch in the pictures of the former Africa are spread over a thousand years in time, a continental unity nevertheless reveals itself. In the thousand years before any serious penetration by Europeans began, though empire succeeded empire, though peoples conquered and peoples moved, though extra-continental influences filtered over the Sahara, and up the Nile, and licked at the coasts, the basic social structure changed very little. An essentially African pattern of society, more often than not organized into essentially African states, had come into being long before any contact with either Christianity or Islam was possible: Whether Christianized as in Ethiopia, or Islamized as in the Sudan, this pattern remained characteristically African. Unfortunately, the tales of the travelers show this unity only in the more superficial details. As today it is the highlights of a journey that one records with the camera—the spectacular and the extraordinary, not the prosaic and the usual—so, in their time, the men who went to report on an unknown continent brought back their well observed pictures, drawn largely from the spectacular and the unusual. And they missed much of the basic reality. The anthologist looking for lively illustrations for such a vast and diverse area tends to accentuate this tendency. The result has been a preponderance of descriptions of the courts of kings, and comparatively little of African life away from the centers of power, or in the stateless societies that also existed. The court-sponsored, orally transmitted history of Africa, like indeed most other history, makes the same selection of subject matter. In this way the two fundamental aspects of society that make a surprisingly well-knit unit of Negro Africa are scarcely shown. The first is the extended family system which ties, in varying ways, the whole range of cousinship into a closely integrated family circle, with specific rights inherent in the kinship. The second is the underlying concept of almost all African religion: that the mediators between a living man and an infinitely remote Almighty Being are his long line of ancestors. For these things the reader must go to the scientific works of anthropologists. He will find them neither in the superficial accounts of travelers nor in the oral tradition which took them for granted.

Nonetheless, in their own way, the diverse accounts of the courts of kings collected in this anthology give evidence of a continental unity. The sacred, absolute monarchy, which African man accepted and presumably chose, as well as the pattern of states both great and small, is found throughout the continent. The rites which bolstered despotism recur with great consistency of detail and show clearly a common origin.

At times the traveler's camera has highlighted the cruelty that was involved in the rites of sacred monarchy. The non-African reader, from his privileged position in time, must be careful not to criticize. The tale of cruelty is universal. The Inquisition is a horrid chapter in the history of Christianity. In the year that Sir Richard Burton witnessed the human sacrificial rites in Dahomey, a hundred thousand Englishmen watched a multiple public hanging in Liverpool. The torture of European Jewry in our own times is, in its way, more horrible than anything recorded here. The African reader may dislike the way in which this kind of anthology throws the cruelty into relief, but these sacred rites loomed large in the life of bygone Africa, and cannot be ignored. No more than all the other peoples of the world can Africans escape the common heritage of man's inhumanity to man.

Part I of this collection concerns that part of Africa which has come to be known as West Africa. Geographically, this consists of a wide savannah belt immediately south of the Sahara Desert, and a further wide belt of forest between the Savannah and the Guinea coast of the Atlantic.

In the savannah belt, known to the Arabs of North Africa as the Sudan, or "Land of the Blacks," flourished a number of powerful Negro empires which are fairly well documented from about the tenth century. The states of Ghana, Mali, Songhai, the Hausa states, and Kanem-Bornu (extracts 1 to 7) are the outstanding examples.

The political concept of these Sudanic states, that of divine kingship, was possibly derived from the kingdom of Meroe in the Upper Nile valley. Meroe, which lasted from early in the first millennium B.C. until the middle of the fourth century A.D., was itself strongly influenced by Egyptian and Southwest Asian ideas. The available evidence points to trading or military groups from Meroe who dispersed westward from time to time, and imposed their political organization on the agricultural Negroes of the savannah belt. As there is at present no evidence of contact between West Africa and similar states in East and Central Africa, it seems that the political ideas of Meroe flowed out in two streams, the one westerly, the other southerly.

In Islamic times, the Sudanic states were in contact across the Sahara with the Arab civilization of North Africa, and from this derives the documentation. Ambassadors from North African sultanates and, frequently, Muslim scholars traveled with the merchants who plied the caravan roads of the Sahara. Many scholars settled there, and great centers of Muslim learning, closely linked with the Muslim world, grew up in Sudanic trading cities such as Timbuktu and Jenne. The libraries of Timbuktu attracted Imams from afar, and Jenne was especially noted for Negro scholars.

The next extracts (8 to 13) refer to the states of the West African forest belt. These were strongly influenced by the Sudanic states, but unforunately no Muslim from across the Sahara has left an account of any of them, and their existence is undocumented until the arrival of the Portuguese on the Guinea coast at the end of the fifteenth century. With the exceptions of Benin and Dahomey, it was not until the nineteenth century that Europeans penetrated far enough inland to have any first-hand knowledge, but on such evidence as exists, mainly that of oral tradition, we know that many of the forest states had taken shape by the end of the thirteenth century. They were most probably founded, according to the usual African pattern, by immigrants from the Sudan, probably refugees from Islam, who imposed their superior political skill on the forest peoples. They certainly had close trading links with the Sudan and therefore, indirectly, with North Africa, until the European slave trade on the Guinea coast reoriented the West African economy and changed the balance of power between the Sudan and the forest. The states to the east of the Volta, such as the Yoruba states and Benin and Dahomey, descend either from the Hausa states or from the great empire of Kanem-Bornu. Those to the west of the Volta, such as Ashanti, descend from ancient Ghana and ancient Mali.

Despite the obscurity of their history, there was one remarkable happening in the forest states, for which there is abundant evidence. This was the great flowering of the art of sculpture in Ife and Benin, which probably reached its height in the fourteenth or fifteenth century. Superb examples of this art are still in existence, and without doubt they rank with the greatest sculptures of the world. Practically nothing is known of the society that produced this astonishing culture. The elaborate techniques of brass-casting probably came from the Nile valley, but the evidence suggests that the ancestry of the art itself was comparatively local.

Part II of the collection, which covers the rest of Africa, does not show the same cohesion as has been shown in West Africa, which, except for a common political heritage from the Nile valley, is historically separate from the rest of Negro Africa. The cohesion which characterized West Africa can be found, outside West Africa, only in the Nile valley and in Ethiopia, which have their own histories.

Though Meroe was the filter through which the political organization of the Pharoahs passed to so much of Africa, the history of the Nile valley is not directly that of Negro Africa. In its later centuries, the population of Meroe, the center of which had moved south in the course of its history, was largely Negro. The successors to Meroe were the Nubian kingdoms which were Christianized from Egypt late in the sixth century, and resisted the advance of Islam for four hundred years. Part II begins with a contemporary account of these kingdoms (extract 15).

The next four selections (extracts 16 to 19) describe Ethiopia, of which the comparatively well documented history stands apart, as far as is known, from the rest of Negro Africa. Axum, the core of the complex conglomeration of states comprising Ethiopia, was evangelized from Egypt and Syria in the early years of Christianity, and has remained largely Christian and in contact with the Egyptian Coptic Church to the present day. For a time, before the coming of Islam, it exerted its dominance beyond the Red Sea into South Arabia. Although close to the heart of Islam, the great tide of Islamic expansion bypassed it, and subsequent threats from Islam were circumvented.

Like the West African states, the Ethiopian political system was, and is, that of divine kingship. Accounts of the monarchy and the court show features in common with West African courts, notably Kanem-Bornu. This indicates a common heritage from Meroe, but Ethiopia was also directly influenced from Asia. It is possible that Ethiopia was another route by which Egyptian and Asian influences reached down into Central Africa, but there is no evidence in support of this.

The remaining extracts refer to Bantu Africa, that is, the substantial two thirds of Negro Africa where the several hundred languages of the Bantu language family are spoken. Here, too, organized states ruled by sacred despots flourished, but here, as far as the evidence goes, they flourished for many centuries free from extraneous influences. Even the route by which the basic idea of kingship reached them is unknown. But it cannot be mere coincidence that, for example, the sultan of Bornu, the emperor of Ethiopia, and the Monomotapa in his kingdom to the south of the Zambezi were all screened from the public gaze when giving audience.

For the most part, the largest of these states are strung out along the highland spine of Africa where climatic conditions and vegetation are conducive to population density. Where a prosperous court employed oral historians, the more recent history of the dominant states can be largely recovered. Where a number of organized states are grouped together, as, for instance, in the lake regions of East Africa (extracts 20 to 26), the history of the area can be partially reconstructed for as much as five hundred years past. But the migrations and fusions of peoples which originally brought these state systems into being are completely obscure. From archaeological evidence it appears that the copper of the Katanga was being mined and worked with fairly advanced techniques in the eighth or ninth centuries A.D. This evidence is associated with the virile Luba people who lived and still live in the area. It is known from oral tradition that the Luba spread their influence both westward over the Lunda peoples (extract 31) and southeastward over the Marave peoples (extracts 32, 33). The Jagas (extract 28) were also of Luba origin. Presumably the good living conditions in the uplands, where the Congo and Zambezi rise, led to a continuous overflow into the surrounding regions. It is possible that, at second hand, this diffusion of comparatively skilled people led in time to the founding of the Shona states, such as those of the Monomotapa and the Kiteve (extracts 32, 33), but this is unsubstantiated.

In the absence of any integrating historical facts, the anthologist can only draw aside, here and there, the curtain which conceals the lives of the peoples of Bantu Africa who were for long ages cut off from the main stream of history by the formidable barriers between the uplands and the coasts—impenetrable forests, the swamps of the upper Nile, and the tsetse fly.

As the object of this collection is to illustrate the Africa of the past, the more personal details of the travelers' comfort, sufferings, or relationships have been generally omitted from the texts of travel narratives. The travelers' personalities, nonetheless, show themselves sufficiently for the reader to touch in for himself, if only lightly, a picture of the whole great company of African adventurers, spread over the centuries; Muslim theologian, ship-wrecked sailor, Portuguese priest, Scottish laird, English country gentleman, shared alike the curiosity, the courage, and the competence necessary for their journeys. They were sometimes ludicrously proud. They were often smug, superior, and censorious. But their narratives, written down after arduous marches, in conditions of physical discomfort and even danger, frequently reveal a sympathetic understanding of the peoples they encountered, whose way of life was so different from their own.

PART I

1 / ANCIENT GHANA AND THE CUSTOMS OF ITS INHABITANTS

The first description known to exist of the western Sudan was that included by Al Bakri in his great general geographical work, Roads and Kingdoms. *Al Bakri, a member of a Spanish Arab family of distinction, was born in 1028 in Cordova, then a center of Muslim learning. Although he never left Spain, the accuracy of his geography suggests that he had access to good documentation. The close links between Moorish Spain and North Africa, with its trans-Saharan trade, would have brought him into contact with travelers who had visited the Sudan. Only a part of his monumental work survives, but that part includes his writings on both North and West Africa.*

His description of ancient Ghana is important, being nearly contemporary to its greatest days in the tenth century. Geographically, ancient Ghana, as far as is known the first of the western Sudanic empires, lay with its center about a thousand miles to the northwest of modern Ghana. It was populated by the Mande, as was the Mali empire, with its center to the east, in the Niger valley, which eventually succeeded it as the great power of the western Sudan.

. . . Ghana is also the title given to their kings; the name of the region is Awkar, and their king today, namely in A.H. 460 [i.e.,

Al Bakri, *Roads and Kingdoms.* Translated (unpublished) by Dr. W. W. Rajkowski. From "Ancient Ghana: A Review of the Evidence," by J. D. Fage, in *Transactions of the Historical Society of Ghana* (Achimota, 1952), Vol. III, pp. 80-82. Reprinted by permission of the publisher.

A.D. 1067-68], *is Tankamanin*. . . . The name of the previous king was Basi. . . . He led a praiseworthy life on account of his love of justice and his friendship for the Muslims. At the end of his life he became blind, but he concealed this from his subjects and pretended that he could see. When something was put before him, he said "This is good" or "This is bad." His ministers deceived the people by telling the king what he had to say in cryptic language so that the commoners could not understand. Basi was a maternal uncle to Tankamanin. This is their custom and their usage. The kingdom is inherited only by the son of the king's sister. He has no doubts that his successor is a son of his sister, while he is not certain that his son is in fact his own, and he does not rely on the genuineness of this relationship. This Tankamanin is powerful, rules an enormous kingdom, and possesses great authority.

The city of Ghana consists of two towns lying in a plain. One of these towns is inhabited by Muslims. It is large and possesses twelve mosques in one of which the people assemble for the Friday prayer. There are imams, muezzins, and assistants as well as jurists and learned men. Around the town are wells of sweet water from which they drink and near which they grow vegetables. The town in which the king lives is six miles from the Muslim one and bears the name Al Ghaba.[1] The land between the two towns is covered with houses. The houses of the inhabitants are made of stone and acacia wood. The king has a palace and a number of dome-shaped dwellings, the whole surrounded by an enclosure like the defensive wall of a city. In the town where the king lives, and not far from the hall where he holds his court of justice, is a mosque where pray the Muslims who come on visiting diplomatic missions. Around the king's town are domed buildings, woods, and copses where live the sorcerers of these people, the men in charge of the religious cult. In these also are idols and the tombs of their kings. These woods are guarded and no unauthorized person can enter them, so that it is not known what is within them. In them also are the prisons of the king, and if anyone is imprisoned there, no more is ever heard of him. The king's interpreters, his treasurer, and the majority of his ministers, are Muslims.

Of the people who follow the king's religion, only he and his heir presumptive, who is the son of his sister, may wear sewn

[1] The forest.

clothes. All other people wear cloths of cotton, silk, or brocade, according to their means. All men shave their beards and women shave their heads. The king adorns himself like a woman, wearing necklaces and bracelets, and when he sits before the people he puts on a high cap decorated with gold and wrapped in turbans of fine cotton. The court of appeal is held in a domed pavilion around which stand ten horses with gold embroidered trappings. Behind the king stand ten pages holding shields and swords decorated with gold, and on his right are the sons of the subordinate kings of his country, all wearing splendid garments and with their hair mixed with gold. The governor of the city sits on the ground before the king, and around him are ministers seated likewise. At the door of the pavilion are dogs, of excellent pedigree which, guarding the king, hardly ever leave the place where he is. Round their necks they wear collars of gold and silver, studded with a number of balls of the same metals. The audience is announced by the beating of a drum which they call *daba,* made from a long hollow log. When the people who profess the same religion as the king approach him, they fall on their knees and sprinkle their heads with dust, for this is their way of showing him their respect. As for the Muslims, they greet him only by clapping their hands.

The religion of the people of Ghana is paganism and the worship of idols. When their king dies they build, over the place where his tomb will be, an enormous dome of *saj* wood. Then they bring him on a bed covered with a few carpets and cushions and put him inside the dome. At his side they place his ornaments, his weapons, and the vessels from which he used to eat and drink, filled with various kinds of food and beverages. They also place there the men who have served his meals. They close the door of the dome and cover it with mats and materials, and then they assemble the people, who heap earth upon it until it becomes like a large mound. Then they dig a ditch around the mound so that it can be reached only at one place. They sacrifice victims for their dead and make offerings of intoxicating drinks.

For every donkey loaded with salt that enters the country, the king takes a duty of one golden *dinar,*[2] and two *dinars* from every one that leaves. From a load of copper the duty due to the king is

[2] About ⅛ oz. of gold.

five *mithqals*,[3] and from a load of merchandise ten *mithqals*. The best gold found in this land comes from the town of Ghiyaru, which is eighteen days traveling from the city of the king, over a country inhabited by tribes of the Negroes, their dwelling places being contiguous. The nuggets found in all the mines of this country are reserved for the king, only gold dust being left for the people. Without this precaution, the people would accumulate gold until it had lost its value. The nuggets may be of any weight from an ounce to a pound. It is said that the king owns a nugget as large as a big stone. The town of Ghiyaru is twelve miles from the Nile [i.e., the Niger] and contains many Muslims.

The countryside of Ghana is unhealthy and not populous, and it is almost impossible to avoid falling ill there at the season when their crops are growing. The mortality among strangers is highest at the time of the harvest. . . . When the king of Ghana calls up his army, he can put 200,000 men in the field, more than 40,000 of whom are bowmen. The horses in Ghana are very small.

2 / IBN BATTUTA IN THE NEGROLANDS

Ibn Battuta, a North African Berber, was born in Tangier in 1304. At the age of twenty-one he departed on the customary pilgrimage to Mecca. In the twenty-four years before he returned home, he traveled widely throughout the known world. His early education in Tangier had been that of a Muslim theologian, and three more years of study in Mecca made him a scholar of some repute. This fame preceded him on his journey and facilitated his way through the Middle East, India, Ceylon, Assam, and many other places. Peking was the outward limit of his journey. He returned to Tangier in 1349, and in 1352, in order to complete his tour of the Muslim world, he set out southward across the Sahara. The narrative of this journey, which he dictated on his return to Tangier, is, in spite of some inaccuracy, of great value. Especially important is the contemporary account it gives of Mali, which had replaced Ghana in the early thirteenth century as the dominating empire of the western Sudan. In the extracts from the narrative given here, the description of Mali is preceded by one of Walata, then a dependency of Mali with a Negro governor. It was in this important

---

[3] One *mithqal* also equals ⅛ oz. of gold.

*center of commerce and of learning that he first came in contact
with the Negro world.*

At Sijilmasa[1] I bought camels and a four months' supply of forage
for them. Thereupon I set out on the 1st Muharram of the year
seven hundred and fifty-three [18th February 1352] with a caravan
including, amongst others, a number of the merchants of Sijilmasa.
After twenty-five days we reached Taghaza,[2] an unattractive village,
with the curious feature that its houses and mosques are built of
blocks of salt, roofed with camel skins. There are no trees there,
nothing but sand. In the sand is a salt mine; they dig for the salt,
and find it in thick slabs, lying one on top of the other, as though
they had been tool-squared and laid under the surface of the earth.
A camel will carry two of these slabs. No one lives at Taghaza
except the slaves of the Masufa tribe, who dig for the salt; they
subsist on dates imported from Dara[3] and Sijilmasa, camel's flesh,
and millet imported from the Negrolands. The Negroes come up
from their country and take away the salt from there. At Walata
a load of salt brings eight to ten *mithqals;* in the town of Mali it
sells for twenty to thirty, and sometimes as much as forty. The
Negroes use salt as a medium of exchange, just as gold and silver
is used elsewhere; they cut it up into pieces, and buy and sell with
it. The business done at Taghaza, for all its meanness, amounts to
an enormous figure in terms of hundredweights of gold dust. . . .

Thus we reached the town of Walata after a journey of two
months to a day. Walata is the northernmost province of the Negroes, and the sultan's representative there was one Farba Husayn,
farba meaning deputy [in their language]. When we arrived there,
the merchants deposited their goods in an open square, where the
blacks undertook to guard them, and went to the *farba.* He was
sitting on a carpet under an archway, with his guards before him
carrying lances and bows in their hands, and the headman of the
Masufa behind him. The merchants remained standing in front of
him while he spoke to them through an interpreter, although they

Ibn Battuta. Translated by H. A. R. Gibb. From *Travels of Ibn Battuta in
Asia and Africa,* by H. A. R. Gibb (London: Routledge & Kegan Paul, Ltd.,
1927), Chap. IV, pp. 317-31. Reprinted by permission of Routledge & Kegan
Paul, Ltd.

[1] Principal trading station south of the Atlas, near modern Tafilelt.

[2] Important outpost of the Negro empires.

[3] The Wadi Dra which drains the southern slopes of the anti-Atlas mountains.

were close to him, to show his contempt for them.[4] It was then that I repented of having come to their country, because of their lack of manners and their contempt for the whites. . . .

Later on the *mushrif* [inspector] of Walata, whose name was Mansa Ju, invited all those who had come with the caravan to partake of his hospitality. At first I refused to attend, but my companions urged me very strongly, so I went with the rest. The repast was served—some pounded millet mixed with a little honey and milk, put in a half calabash shaped like a large bowl. The guests drank and retired. I said to them, "Was it for this that the black invited us?" They answered, "Yes; and it is in their opinion the highest form of hospitality." This convinced me that there was no good to be hoped for from these people, and I made up my mind to travel back to Morocco at once with the pilgrim caravan from Walata. Afterwards, however, I thought it best to go to see the capital of their king [at Mali]. My stay at Walata lasted about fifty days; and I was shown honor and entertained by its inhabitants. It is an excessively hot place, and boasts a few small date-palms, in the shade of which they sow watermelons. Its water comes from underground water beds at that point, and there is plenty of mutton to be had. The garments of the inhabitants, most of whom belong to the Masufa tribe, are of fine Egyptian fabrics. Their women are of surpassing beauty, and are shown more respect than the men. The state of affairs amongst these people is indeed extraordinary. Their men show no sign of jealousy whatever; no one claims descent from his father, but on the contrary from his mother's brother. A person's heirs are his sister's sons, not his own sons. This is a thing which I have seen nowhere in the world except among the Indians of Malabar. But those are heathens; *these* people are Muslims, punctilious in observing the hours of prayer, studying books of law, and memorizing the Koran. Yet their women show no bashfulness before men and do not veil themselves, though they are assiduous in attending prayers. Any man who wishes to marry one of them may do so, but they do not travel with their husbands, and, even if one desired to do so, her family would not allow her to go.

[4] It was common practice in West Africa for rulers to communicate only through the medium of an official "interpreter," who relayed the speech backward and forward. There was a similar practice at the Ethiopian court.

The women have their "friends" and "companions" amongst the men outside their own families, and the men in the same way have "companions" amongst the women of other families. A man may go into his house and find his wife entertaining her "companion" but he takes no objection to it. One day at Walata I went into the qadi's[5] house, after asking his permission to enter, and found with him a young woman of remarkable beauty. When I saw her I was shocked and turned to go out, but she laughed at me, instead of being overcome by shame, and the qadi said to me, "Why are you going out? She is my companion." I was amazed at their conduct, for he was a theologian and a pilgrim to boot. I was told that he had asked the sultan's permission to make the pilgrimage that year with his "companion" (whether this one or not I cannot say) but the sultan would not grant it.

When I decided to make the journey to Mali, which is reached in twenty-four days from Walata if the traveler pushes on rapidly, I hired a guide from the Masufa (for there is no necessity to travel in company on account of the safety of that road), and set out with three of my companions. On the way there are many trees, and these trees are of great age and girth; a whole caravan may shelter in the shade of one of them. There are trees[6] which have neither branches nor leaves, yet the shade cast by their trunks is sufficient to shelter a man. Some of these trees are rotted in the interior and the rain water collects in them, so that they serve as wells, and the people drink of the water inside them. In others there are bees and honey, which is collected by the people. I was surprised to find inside one tree, by which I passed, a man, a weaver, who had set up his loom in it and was actually weaving.

A traveler in this country carries no provisions, whether plain food or seasonings, and neither gold nor silver. He takes nothing but pieces of salt and glass ornaments, which the people call beads, and some aromatic goods. When he comes to a village the women-folk of the blacks bring out millet, milk, chickens, pulped lotus fruit, rice, *funi* (a grain resembling mustard seed, from which *kuskusu*[7] and gruel are made), and pounded haricot beans. The

---

[5] Qadi: a Muslim judge.

[6] Baobab trees.

[7] Cereal dish of Northwest Africa made from coarsely ground flour.

traveler buys what of these he wants, but their rice causes sickness to whites when it is eaten, and the *funi* is preferable to it. . . .

Ten days after leaving Walata we came to the village of Zaghari, a large village, inhabited by Negro traders called *wanjarati*,[8] along with whom live a community of whites of the Ibadite sect. It is from this village that the millet is carried to Walata. After leaving Zaghari we came to the great river, that is the Nile,[9] on which stands the town of Karsakhu. The Nile flows from there down to Kabara, and thence to Zagha. In both Kabara and Zagha there are sultans who owe allegiance to the king of Mali. The inhabitants of Zagha are of old standing in Islam; they show a great devotion and zeal for study. Thence the Nile descends to Timbuktu and Gao, both of which will be described later; then to the town of Muli in the land of the Limis, which is the frontier province of [the kingdom of] Mali; thence to Nupe, one of the largest towns of the Negroes, whose ruler is one of the most considerable of the Negro rulers. It cannot be visited by any white man because they would kill him before he got there. . . .

I saw a crocodile in this part of the Nile, close to the bank; it looked just like a small boat. One day I went down to the river to satisfy a need, and lo, one of the blacks came and stood between me and the river. I was amazed at such lack of manners and decency on his part, and spoke of it to someone or other. He answered, "His purpose in doing that was solely to protect you from the crocodile, by placing himself between you and it."

We set out thereafter from Karsakhu and came to the river of Sansara, which is about ten miles from Mali. It is their custom that no persons except those who have obtained permission are allowed to enter the city. I had already written to the white community [there] requesting them to hire a house for me, so when I arrived at the river, I crossed by the ferry without interference. Thus I reached the city of Mali, the capital of the king of the blacks. . . .

The sultan of Mali is Mansa Sulayman, *mansa* meaning [in Mande] sultan, and Sulayman being his proper name. He is a miserly king, not a man from who one might hope for a rich present. . . .

[8] Wangara traders from Mali.
[9] It was, of course, not the Nile but the Niger.

On certain days the sultan holds audiences in the palace yard, where there is a platform under a tree, with three steps; this they call the *pempi*. It is carpeted with silk, and has cushions placed on it. [Over it] is raised the umbrella, which is a sort of pavilion made of silk, surmounted by a bird of gold, about the size of a falcon. The sultan comes out of a door in a corner of the palace, carrying a bow in his hand and a quiver on his back. On his head he has a golden skullcap, bound with a gold band which has narrow ends shaped like knives, more than a span in length. His usual dress is a velvety red tunic, made of the European fabrics called *mutanfas*. The sultan is preceded by his musicians, who carry gold and silver *guimbris* [two-stringed guitars], and behind him come three hundred armed slaves. He walks in a leisurely fashion, affecting a very slow movement, and even stops from time to time. On reaching the *pempi* he stops and looks round the assembly, then ascends it in the sedate manner of a preacher ascending a mosque pulpit. As he takes his seat the drums, trumpets, and bugles are sounded. Three slaves go out at a run to summon the sovereign's deputy and the military commanders, who enter and sit down. Two saddled and bridled horses are brought, along with two goats, which they hold to serve as a protection against the evil eye. Dugha stands at the gate, and the rest of the people remain in the street under the trees.

The Negroes are, of all people, the most submissive to their king and the most abject in their behavior before him. They swear by his name, saying, "Mansa Sulayman ki." [10] If he summons any of them while he is holding an audience in the pavilion, the person summoned takes off his clothes and puts on worn garments, removes his turban and dons a dirty skullcap, and enters with his garments and trousers raised knee-high. He goes forward in an attitude of humility and dejection, and knocks the ground hard with his elbows, then stands with bowed head and bent back listening to what he says. If anyone addresses the king and receives a reply from him, he uncovers his back and throws dust over his head and back, for all the world like a bather splashing himself with water. I used to wonder how it was they did not blind themselves. If the sultan delivers any remarks during his audience, those present take off their turbans and put them down, and listen to what he says.

[10] "The Emperor Sulayman has commanded," in Mandingo.

Sometimes one of them stands up before him and recalls his deeds in the sultan's service, saying "I did so-and-so on such a day," or, "I killed so-and-so on such a day." Those who have knowledge of this confirm his words, which they do by plucking the cord of the bow and releasing it with a twang, just as an archer does when shooting an arrow. If the sultan says, "Truly spoken," or thanks him, he removes his clothes and "dusts." That is their idea of good manners. . . .

I was at Mali during the two festivals of the sacrifice and the fast-breaking. On these days the sultan takes his seat on the *pempi* after the mid-afternoon prayer. The armor-bearers bring in magnificent arms—quivers of gold and silver, swords ornamented with gold and with golden scabbards, gold and silver lances, and crystal maces. At his head stand four *amirs* driving off the flies, having in their hands silver ornaments resembling saddle stirrups. The commanders, qadi, and preacher sit in their usual places. The interpreter Dugha comes with his four wives and his slave-girls, who are about a hundred in number. They are wearing beautiful robes, and on their heads they have gold and silver fillets, with gold and silver balls attached. A chair is placed for Dugha to sit on. He plays on an instrument made of reeds, with some small calabashes at its lower end, and chants a poem in praise of the sultan, recalling his battles and deeds of valor. The women and girls sing along with him and play with bows. Accompanying them are about thirty youths, wearing red woollen tunics and white skullcaps; each of them has a drum slung from his shoulder and beats it. Afterward come his boy pupils who play and turn wheels in the air, like the natives of Sind. They show a marvelous nimbleness and agility in these exercises, and play most cleverly with swords. Dugha makes a fine play with the sword. Thereupon the sultan orders a gift to be presented to Dugha and he is given a purse containing two hundred *mithqals* of gold dust, and is informed of the contents of the purse before all the people. The commanders rise and twang their bows in thanks to the sultan. The next day each one of them gives Dugha a gift, every man according to his rank. Every Friday after the *'asr* prayer, Dugha carries out a similar ceremony to this that we have described.

On feast-days, after Dugha has finished his display, the poets come in. Each of them is inside a figure resembling a thrush, made of feathers, and provided with a wooden head with a red beak, to look like a thrush's head. They stand in front of the sultan in this ridiculous make-up and recite their poems. I was told that their poetry is a kind of sermonizing in which they say to the sultan: "This *pempi* which you occupy was that whereon sat this king and that king, and such were this one's noble actions and such and such the other's. So do you too do good deeds whose memory will outlive you." After that the chief of the poets mounts the steps of the *pempi* and lays his head on the sultan's lap, then climbs to the top of the *pempi* and lays his head first on the sultan's right shoulder and then on his left, speaking all the while in their tongue, and finally he comes down again. I was told that this practice is a very old custom amongst them, prior to the introduction of Islam, and that they have kept it up.

The Negroes disliked Mansa Sulayman because of his avarice. His predecessor was Mansa Magha, and before him reigned Mansa Musa, a generous and virtuous prince, who loved the whites and made gifts to them. It was he who gave Ibn Ishaq as-Sahili four thousand *mithqals* in the course of a single day. I heard from a truthworthy source that he gave three thousand *mithqals* on one day to Mudrik ibn Faqqus, by whose grandfather his own grandfather, Saraq Jata, had been converted to Islam.

The Negroes possess some admirable qualities. They are seldom unjust, and have a greater abhorrence of injustice than any other people. The sultan shows no mercy to anyone who is guilty of the least act of it. There is complete security in their country. Neither traveler nor inhabitant in it has anything to fear from robbers or men of violence. They do not confiscate the property of any white man who dies in their country, even if it be accounted wealth. On the contrary, they give it into the charge of some trustworthy person among the whites, until the rightful heir takes possession of it. They are careful to observe the hours of prayer, and assiduous in attending them in congregations, and in bringing up their children to them. On Fridays, if a man does not go early to the mosque, he cannot find a corner to pray in, on account of the crowd. It is a custom of theirs to send each man his boy [to the mosque] with his prayer-mat; the boy spreads it out for his master in a place befitting him and remains on it [until his master comes to the mosque]. The prayer-mats are made of the leaves of a tree resembling a date-palm, but without fruit.

Another of their good qualities is their habit of wearing clean white garments on Fridays. Even if a man has nothing but an old worn shirt, he washes it and cleans it, and wears it at the Friday service. Yet another is their zeal for learning the Koran by heart. They put their children in chains if they show any backwardness in memorizing it, and they are not set free until they have it by heart. I visited the qadi in his house on the day of the festival. His children were chained up, so I said to him, "Will you not let them loose?" He replied, "I shall not do so until they learn the Koran by heart." Among their bad qualities are the following. The women servants, slave-girls, and young girls go about in front of everyone naked, without a stitch of clothing on them. Women go into the sultan's presence naked and without coverings, and his daughters also go about naked. Then there is the custom of their putting dust and ashes on their heads as a mark of respect, and the grotesque ceremonies we have described when the poets recite their verses. Another reprehensible practice among many of them is the eating of carrion, dogs, and asses.

3 / THE FOUNDING OF TIMBUKTU

Es Sadi, the author of the Tarikh es Sudan, *from which this extract is taken, belonged to an aristocratic family of Timbuktu, where he was born in 1596. Imam of both Timbuktu and Jenne in the course of his life, he was especially devoted to the former, at that time the greatest city of the Negrolands and the capital of the Moorish Sudanic Empire. The Songhai Empire, with Gao as capital and Timbuktu as a subsidiary capital, started to supersede the Mali Empire in the late fourteenth century. Its history is the subject of the first part of the* Tarikh, *which then goes on to give an account, compiled from sources not now extant, of the Moorish invasion. Finally it deals with contemporary history in which Es Sadi himself was taking part. In the seventeenth century, Moorish armies exercised an unruly domination over the Niger states. Timbuktu was still a center of learning, mainly for Berber scholars, while Jenne,*

Es Sadi, *Tarikh es Sudan.* From the French translation by O. Houdas (Paris, 1900), pp. 35-38. Translated from the French by Caroline Oliver.

*the other city where Es Sadi worked, was the center for Negro
scholars. Es Sadi's history ends in 1655, presumably because of the
author's death.*

The town was founded by the Maghsharen Tuareg at the end
of the fifth century of the Hegira [c. 1200 A.D.]. They came to the
region to graze their herds. In the summer season they used to
camp on the banks of the Niger in the village of Amazagha. In the
autumn they returned to Aruan where they lived. It was their
extreme limit in the highland regions. They actually chose the
site which is occupied by this exquisite, pure, charming, celebrated,
blessed, rich, and gay city, which is my birthplace, and that which
I hold dearest in all the world.

Never has Timbuktu been profaned by the worship of idols. On
its soil no one has ever knelt but to the Merciful. It is the refuge
of the learned and the devout, the habitual dwelling place of
saints and pious men.

At first it was the meeting place of travelers coming by land or
water. They made there a warehouse for their tackle and grain.
Soon the place became a crossroads for travelers who passed
through going to and fro. They entrusted the care of their effects
to a female slave called Timbuktu, a word which in the vernacular
means "the ancient one." It is from her that the blessed spot has
taken its name.

Later on, the place where by God's will people went to cross the
river began to be residential. They came there from all parts, and
soon it became a center of commerce. To begin with it was the
people of Wagadu who came to trade in the greatest numbers.
Later traders came from all the neighboring regions.

Formerly, the center of commerce was at Biru.[1] The caravans of
all nations flowed there, and great scholars and pious persons and
rich men of all races and all countries settled there. They came
from Egypt, Awdjela, Fezzan, Ghadames, Tuat, Dana, Tafilelt, Fez,
Sus, Bitu, etc.

All this transferred itself little by little to Timbuktu, and ended
by being concentrated there entirely. The tribes of the Sanhadja
added themselves to the population as well. The prosperity of

[1] Walata.

Timbuktu was the ruin of Biru. Its civilization came to it entirely from the Maghrib, both as regards religion and commerce.

At first the dwellings of the inhabitants consisted of straw huts in thorn enclosures, and then they changed to mud huts. Eventually the town was enclosed with very low mud walls, of a kind which enabled you to see from the outside what was going on inside. They next built a big mosque, sufficient for their needs, and then the Sankore mosque. Anyone standing at the city gate at that time could see those who were entering the big mosque, as then the town had few walls and buildings. It was only at the end of the ninth century [of the Hegira] that the prosperity of the town finally sprang to life. The dense medley of buildings was not completed till the middle of the tenth century [of the Hegira] in the reign of Askia Daud, son of the Amir Askia-el-Hajji-Muhammad. As has already been said, the first dynasty to reign in Timbuktu was that of the people of Mali. It lasted a hundred years starting from 737 [1336–1337 A.D.]. Following that, the Maghsharen Tuareg ruled for forty years from 837 [1433-1434]. After them came Sonni Ali, whose reign, starting in 873 [1468-1469], lasted twenty-four years. It was replaced by the Prince of Believers, Askia-el-Hajji-Muhammad, whose reign, and that of his successors, lasted a hundred-and-one years, from the 14th Djumada II of the year 898, to the 17th Djumada II of the year 999 [2nd April 1493-12th April 1591]. Finally the power fell to the Hashimite ruler, the Sultan Mulay Ahmad adh Dhahabi [of Morocco] whose domination began with the fall of the Songhai dynasty, that is to say, on the 17th Djumada II 999 [12th April 1591]. Today it is sixty-five years since the reign of this prince and his successors began.

4 / TIMBUKTU IN 1526

Leo Africanus, whose real name was Al Hassan Ibn Muhammad, was born in Granada about 1495, not long after its capture by Ferdinand and Isabella. His parents, like many Spanish Moors of the time, crossed to Africa and settled near Fez. Both Fez and Marrakesh were then great centers of Muslim learning, and he was very well educated.

From Leo Africanus, *The History and Description of Africa done into English by John Pory* (London: Hakluyt Society, 1896), pp. 824-26.

In 1513 he departed southward on the much used route of the trans-Saharan merchants, accompanying his uncle who was on a mission from the sultan of Fez to Askia the Great of Songhai.[1] While south of the Sahara they made a prolonged stay at Timbuktu where Askia then had his headquarters, and traveled extensively, visiting fifteen Sudanic states—for the most part, those strung out along the Niger. For all the brilliance of the description of West Africa that Leo was subsequently to give the world, he made a notorious blunder in ascribing to the river a westerly course. Timbuktu and Gao, the Songhai capital, were then booming with the wealth that resulted from Askia's great conquests, and Leo was enormously impressed by the Negro court and the intellectual life of Timbuktu, which flourished under Askia's patronage.

After his return from West Africa he continued to travel widely, and was captured by Christian pirates in 1520, while returning from a voyage to Constantinople. The pirates took their distinguished prisoner to Rome, where the Medici Pope, Leo X, took great delight in the company of the much-traveled Muslim scholar. He gave him his freedom and a pension which enabled him to settle down to a pleasant scholarly life in Rome, where he learned Italian, Latin, and Greek. He was converted to Christianity and christened Giovanni Leo, but if, as is thought, he eventually returned to Africa, he probably recanted. While living in Rome he wrote his very valuable account of fifteenth-century West Africa. The English translation was first published in 1600.

Here are many shops of artificers and merchants, and especially of such as weave linen and cotton cloth. And hither do the Barbary merchants bring cloth of Europe. All the women of this region, except the maid-servants, go with their faces covered, and sell all necessary victuals. The inhabitants, and especially strangers there residing, are exceeding rich, insomuch that the king that now is, married both his daughters to rich merchants. Here are many wells containing most sweet water; and so often as the river Niger overfloweth, they convey the water thereof by certain sluices into the town. Corn, cattle, milk, and butter this region yieldeth in great abundance: but salt is very scarce here; for it is brought hither by land from Taghaza which is 500 miles distant. When I myself was here, I saw one camel's load of salt sold for 80 ducats. The rich king of Timbuktu hath many plates and sceptres of gold,

[1] See introduction to extract 3.

some whereof weigh 1300 pounds: and he keeps a magnificent and well-furnished court. When he travelleth any whither he rideth upon a camel which is led by some of his noblemen; and so he doth likewise when he goeth forth to warfare, and all his soldiers ride upon horses. Whoever will speak unto this king must first fall down before his feet, and then taking up earth must first sprinkle it upon his own head and shoulders: which custom is ordinarily observed by . . . ambassadors from other princes. He hath always 3000 horsemen, and a number of footmen that shoot poisoned arrows, attending upon him. They have often skirmishes with those that refuse to pay tribute, and so many as they take, they sell unto the merchants of Timbuktu. Here are very few horses bred, and the merchants and courtiers keep certain little nags which they use to travel upon: but their best horses are brought out of Barbary. . . . Here are great store of doctors, judges, priests, and other learned men, that are bountifully maintained at the king's cost and charges, and hither are brought divers manuscripts or written books out of Barbary, which are sold for more money than any other merchandise. The coin of Timbuktu is of gold without any stamp or superscription: but in matters of small value they use certain shells[2] brought hither out of the kingdom of Persia, 400 of which are worth a ducat: and $6\frac{2}{3}$ pieces of their gold coin weigh an ounce. The inhabitants are people of gentle and cheerful disposition, and spend a great part of the night singing and dancing through all the streets of the city. . . .

5 / THE COMING OF ISLAM TO KANO

The city of Kano was one of the centers of the loosely knit Hausa states. Its history is given in great detail, and apparently with considerable accuracy, in the "Chronicle of Kano," a document compiled in the nineteenth century, but evidently based on careful records not now known to exist. The known history of the city, probably a settlement of iron-workers originally, begins, according to the "Chronicle," with an invasion of the Zaghawa, a group of eastern Saharan Berbers. The zenith of its greatness in the fifteenth century was preceded by the arrival of Islam from Mali in the fourteenth.[1]

[2] Cowrie shells.
[1] See extract 2.

Yagi, Son of Tsamia, A.H. 750-787 [A.D. 1349-1385]

The eleventh Sarki [king] was Yagi, called Ali. . . . In Yagi's time
the Wangara came from Mali, bringing Islam. The name of their
leader was Abdurahaman Zaite. . . . When they came they commanded the sarki to observe the times of prayer. He complied and
made Gurdumus his imam [religious teacher], and Lawal his muez-
zin. Awta cut the throats of whatever flesh was eaten. Mandawali
was imam of all the Wangara and of the chief men of Kano. Zaite
was their Qadi. The sarki commanded every town in Kano country
to observe times of prayer. So they all did so. A mosque was built
beneath the sacred tree facing east, and prayers were made at the
five appointed times in it. The Sarkin Garazawa was opposed to
prayer, and when the Muslims after praying had gone home, he
would come with his men and defile the whole mosque and cover
it with filth. Dan Buji was told off to patrol round the mosque with
well-armed men from evening until morning. He kept up a constant halloo. For all that, the pagans tried to win him and his men
over. Some of his men followed the pagans and went away, but he
and the rest refused. The defilement continued till Sheshe said
to Fa Mori, "There is no cure for this but prayer." The people
assented. They gathered together on a Tuesday in the mosque at
the evening hour of prayer and prayed against the pagans until
sunrise. They only came away when the sun was well up. Allah
received graciously the prayers addressed to him. The chief of the
pagans was struck blind that day, and afterward all the pagans who
were present at the defilement—they and all their women. After
this they were all afraid. Yagi turned the chief of the pagans out of
his office and said to him, "Be thou sarki among the blind." In the
days of Yagi, it is said, Sarkin Debbi, Sarkin Dab and Sarkin Geno
brought horses to Kano, but this story is not worth credence.

"The Kano Chronicle." From *Sudanese Memoirs,* by H. R. Palmer (Lagos,
1928), Vol. III, pp. 104-106.

6 / KANEM IN THE TENTH CENTURY

The Zaghawa Berbers[1] were the probable founders of Kanem. Yakut, a thirteenth-century geographer, gives an account of the kingdom of the Zaghawa which he quotes from the works, no longer existing, of Al Muhallabi, a tenth-century writer. The state of Kanem was the nucleus of the Bornu Empire. The kingdom of Kanem, situated northeast of Lake Chad, had its great period during the twelfth and thirteenth centuries. Overrun in the fourteenth century by its eastern neighbor, the kingdom of the Bulala, its rulers retreated to Bornu, the region west of Lake Chad, where they built a new empire which endured until the nineteenth century. Thus, in a sense, the old kingdom of Kanem grew into that of Bornu, which is described in extract 7.

The Zaghawa have two cities, one called Manan and the other Tarazaki. Both are in the first clime, and their latitude is 21°. The kingdom of the Zaghawa is said to be a great kingdom among the kingdoms of the Sudan. On their eastern boundary is the kingdom of the Nuba who are above Upper Egypt. Between them is a distance of ten days' journey. They are many tribes. The length of their land is fifteen days' journey through habitations and cultivations all the way. Their houses are all of gypsum, and also the castle of their king. They respect and worship him to the neglect of Allah the most High; and they falsely imagine that he does not eat food. His people provide his food secretly, bringing it into his houses without it being known whence they bring it. If anyone of his subjects happens to meet the camels carrying it, he is immediately killed on the spot. But he drinks in the presence of the chiefs among his companions. His drink is made from Dhura strengthened with honey. His costume is full trousers of thin wool, and he is wrapped round with fine robes of unlined wool, of silk from silk worms, and of delicate brocade. He has absolute power over his subjects, and appropriates what he will of their belongings. Their cattle are goats and cows and camels and horses. Dhura chiefly is cultivated in their land, and beans; also wheat. Most of the ordi-

Al Muhallabi, a lost tenth century work cited by Yakut in the thirteenth century. From "A History of Dafur," by A. J. Arkell, in *Sudan Notes and Records* (Khartoum), Vol. XXXII, part II, p. 225.

[1] The Zaghawa Berbers were also the founders of Kano. See extract 5

nary people are naked, covering themselves with skins. Their livelihood is in cultivation and breeding cattle; and their religion is the worship of their kings, believing it is they who bring life and death and sickness and health. From the towns of Bilma and Qusba in the land of Kawar it lies southeast.

7 / BORNU IN 1823

In the years 1822, 1823, and 1824, three Englishmen, Major Denham, Captain Clapperton, and Dr. Oudney, going south from Tripoli, carried out an extensive trans-Saharan journey of exploration. In due course they came to Bornu, where the ancient dynasty had recently fallen subject to Al-Amin ibn Muhammad al-Kanemi, known as the shaikh of Bornu, a military adventurer from the eastern Sudan. He had refused the sultanate for himself, but maintained a member of the hereditary royal house as puppet sultan. In addition to the Negro people, the Kanembu, about 15,000 Arabic speaking Shuwas lived in Bornu at the time. The extracts that follow describe the reception of the expedition both by the shaikh and by the sultan, the Bornu army on the march, and the shaikh reviewing his troops.

Arrival at Kukawa[1] and Reception by the Shaikh of Bornu

Our accounts had been so contradictory of the state of this country, that no opinion could be formed as to the real condition or the numbers of its inhabitants. We had been told that the Shaikh's soldiers were a few ragged Negroes armed with spears, who lived upon the plunder of the black Kaffir countries, by which he was surrounded, and which he was enabled to subdue by the assistance of a few Arabs who were in his service; and, again, we had been assured that his forces were not only numerous, but to a certain degree well trained. The degree of credit which might be attached to these reports was nearly balanced in the scales of probability; and we advanced toward the town of Kukawa in a most interesting state of uncertainty, whether we should find its chief at the head

From Dixon Denham and Hugh Clapperton, *Narrative of Travels and Discoveries in Northern and Central Africa*, 3rd edition (London, 1828), pp. 207-212, 231-33, 360-62, 364-66.

[1] Capital of Bornu.

of thousands, or be received by him under a tree, surrounded by a few naked slaves.

These doubts however were quickly removed. I had ridden on, a short distance in front of Boo-Khaloom,[2] with his train of Arabs, all mounted, and dressed out in their best apparel; and from the thickness of the trees, soon lost sight of them, fancying that the road could not be mistaken. I rode still onward, and on approaching a spot less thickly planted, was not a little surprised to see in front of me a body of several thousand cavalry drawn up in a line, and extending right and left quite as far as I could see; and, checking my horse, I awaited the arrival of my party, under the shade of a wide-spreading acacia. The Bornu troops remained quite steady, without noise or confusion; and a few horsemen, who were moving about in front giving directions, were the only persons out of the ranks. On the Arabs appearing in sight, a shout, or yell, was given by the shaikh's people, which rent the air: a blast was blown from their rude instruments of music equally loud, and they moved on to meet Boo-Khaloom and his Arabs. There was an appearance of tact and management in their movements which astonished me. Three separate small bodies, from the center of each flank, kept charging rapidly toward us, to within a few feet of our horses' heads, without checking the speed of their own until the moment of their halt, while the whole body moved onward. These parties were mounted on small but perfect horses, who stopped, and wheeled from their utmost speed with great precision and expertness, shaking their spears over their heads, exclaiming, "Barca! barca! Allah hiakkum cha, alla cheraga!—Blessing! blessing! Sons of your country! Sons of your country!" and returning quickly to the front of the body, in order to repeat the charge. While all this was going on, they closed in their right and left flanks, and surrounded the little body of Arab warriors so completely, as to give the compliment of welcoming them very much the appearance of a declaration of their contempt for their weakness. I am quite sure this was premeditated. We were all so closely pressed as to be nearly smothered, and in some danger from the crowding of the horses and clashing of the spears. Moving on was impossible; and we therefore came to a full stop. Our chief was much

[2] An Arab from Tripoli who accompanied them.

enraged, but it was all to no purpose; he was only answered by shrieks of "Welcome!" and spears most unpleasantly rattled over our heads expressive of the same feeling. This annoyance was not however of long duration. Barca Gana, the shaikh's first general, a Negro of noble aspect, clothed in a figured silk robe, and mounted on a beautiful Mandara horse, made his appearance; and after a little delay, the rear was cleared of those who had pressed in upon us, and we moved on, although but very slowly, from the frequent impediment thrown in our way by these wild equestrians.

The shaikh's Negroes, as they were called, meaning the black chiefs and favorites, all raised to that rank by some deed of bravery, were habited in coats of mail composed of iron chain, which covered them from the throat to the knees, dividing behind, and coming on each side of the horse. Some of them had helmets, or rather skullcaps, of the same metal, with chin-pieces, all sufficiently strong to ward off the shock of a spear. Their horses' heads were also defended by plates of iron, brass, and silver, just leaving sufficient room for the eyes of the animal.

At length, on arriving at the gate of the town, ourselves, Boo-Khaloom, and about a dozen of his followers, were alone allowed to enter the gates; and we proceeded along a wide street completely lined with spearmen on foot, with cavalry in front of them, to the door of the shaikh's residence. Here the horsemen were formed up three deep, and we came to a stand. Some of the chief attendants came out, and after a great many "Barca's! Barca's!" retired, when others performed the same ceremony. We were now again left sitting on our horses in the sun. Boo-Khaloom began to lose all patience, and swore by the bashaw's[3] head that he would return to the tents if he was not immediately admitted. He got, however, no satisfaction but a motion of the hand from one of the chief's, meaning "wait patiently": and I whispered to him the necessity of obeying, as we were hemmed in on all sides, and to retire without permission would have been as difficult as to advance. Barca Gana now appeared, and made a sign that Boo-Khaloom should dismount. We were about to follow his example, when an intimation that Boo-Khaloom was alone to be admitted again fixed us to our saddles. Another half hour at least passed without any news from the interior of the building; when the gates opened,

[3] The ruler of Tripolo was the bashaw.

and the four Englishmen[4] only were called for, and we advanced to the *skiffa* (entrance). Here we were stopped most unceremoniously by the black guards in waiting, and were allowed, one by one only, to ascend a staircase; at the top of which we were again brought to a stand by crossed spears, and the open flat hand of a Negro laid upon our breast. Boo-Khaloom came from the inner chamber, and asked, "If we were prepared to salute the shaikh as we did the bashaw?" We replied "Certainly": which was merely an inclination of the head, and laying the right hand on the heart. He advised our laying our hands also on our heads, but we replied, "The thing is impossible! We had but one manner of salutation for any body, except our own sovereign."

Another parley now took place, but in a minute or two he returned, and we were ushered into the presence of this Shaikh of Spears. We found him in a small dark room, sitting on a carpet, plainly dressed in a blue *tobe* [robe] of Sudan and a shawl turban. Two Negroes were on each side of him, armed with pistols, and on his carpet lay a brace of these instruments. Firearms were hanging in different parts of the room, presents from the bashaw and Mustapha al-Ahmar, the sultan of Fezzan, which are here considered as invaluable. His personal appearance was prepossessing, apparently not more than forty-five or forty-six, with an expressive countenance, and a benevolent smile.

Reception by the Sultan of Bornu

Soon after daylight we were summoned to attend the sultan of Bornu. He received us in an open space in front of the royal residence. We were kept at a considerable distance while his people approached to within about 100 yards, passing first on horse-back; and after dismounting and prostrating themselves before him, they took their places on the ground in front, but with their backs to the royal person, which is the custom of the country. He was seated in a sort of cage of cane or wood, near the door of his garden, on a seat which at the distance appeared to be covered with silk or satin, and through the railing looked upon the assembly before him, who formed a sort of semi-circle extending from his seat to nearly where we were waiting. Nothing could be more absurd and

[4] The fourth Englishman was a wheelwright called Hillman recruited in Malta.

grotesque than some, nay all, of the figures who formed this court. Here was all the outward show of pomp and grandeur, without one particle of the staple commodity, power, to plead its excuse. He reigns and governs by the sufferance of the shaikh: and the better to answer his views, by making him more popular with all parties, the sultan is amused by indulging in all the folly and bigotry of the ancient Negro sovereigns. Large bellies and large heads are indispensable for those who serve the court of Bornu; and those who unfortunately possess not the former by nature, or on whom lustiness will not be forced by cramming, make up the deficiency of protuberance by a wadding, which, as they sit on the horse, gives the belly the curious appearance of hanging over the pummel of the saddle. The eight, ten, and twelve shirts, of different colors, that they wear one over the other, help a little to increase this greatness of person. The head is enveloped in folds of muslin or linen of various colors, though mostly white, so as to deform it as much as possible; and those whose turban seemed to be most studied had the effect of making the head appear completely on one side. Besides this they are hung all over with charms, enclosed in little red leather parcels, strung together. The horse, also, has them round his neck, in front of his head, and about the saddle.

When these courtiers, to the number of about two hundred and sixty or three hundred, had taken their seats in front of the sultan, we were allowed to approach to within about pistol-shot of the spot where he was sitting, and desired to sit down ourselves. The ugliest black that can be imagined, his chief eunuch, the only person who approached the sultan's seat, asked for the presents. Boo-Khaloom's were produced, enclosed in a large shawl, and were carried unopened to the presence. Our glimpse was but a faint one of the sultan, through the lattice-work of his pavilion, sufficient however to see that his turban was larger than any of his subjects' and that his face, from the nose downward, was completely covered. A little to our left, and nearly in front of the sultan, was an extempore declaimer shouting forth praises of his master, with his pedigree; and near him one who bore the long wooden *frumfrum*, on which he ever and anon blew a blast, loud and unmusical. Nothing could be more ridiculous than the appearance of these people squatting down in their places, tottering under the weight and magnitude of their turbans and their bellies, while the thin legs that appeared underneath but ill accorded with the bulk of the other parts.

The Bornu Army on the March

We now commenced our march with the Bornu army, in which but little order is preserved previous to coming near the enemy. Everyone seems to know that at a certain point the assembly is to take place; and the general instructions seem to be to everyone to make the best of his own way. The shaikh takes the lead, and close after him comes the sultan of Bornu, who always attends him on these occasions, although he never fights. The former is preceded by five flags, two green, two striped, and one red, with extracts from the Koran written on them in letters of gold, and attended by about a hundred of his chiefs and favorite slaves. A Negro, high in confidence, rides close behind him, bearing his shield, jacket of mail, and wearing his skullcap of steel; he also bears his arms. Another, mounted on a swift *maherhy*,[5] and fantastically dressed with a straw hat and ostrich feathers, carries his timbral or drum, which it is the greatest misfortune to lose in action. On the expedition which cost the Sultan Denhamah, the late sultan of Bornu, his life, the timbrel and the shaikh were supposed to have fallen in a sudden rush of Baghirmis. Almost everyone near him suffered. The people, however, firmly believe that he was saved by a miracle. They say, "He became invisible; that the Baghirmi chiefs scoured the field, calling out for the shaikh; that his drum sounded at intervals, but could not be seen, any more than their leader." Close in the rear of the *maherhies* follow the eunuchs and the harem. The shaikh takes but three wives, who are mounted, astride, on small trained horses, each led by a boy slave, or eunuch—their heads and figures completely enveloped in brown silk burnooses, and a eunuch riding by the side of each. The sultan of Bornu has five times as many attendants, and his harem is three times as numerous: he is attended, also, by men bearing trumpets (*frum-frum*) of hollow wood, ten and twelve feet long. With these a kind of music is constantly kept up. As this instrument is considered an appendage of royalty alone, the shaikh has no *frumfrums*. The *kaigamma*[6] or standard-bearer, rides in front of him, carrying a

---

[5] A riding camel.
[6] An army commander and provincial governor.

very long pole, hung round, at the top, with strips of leather and silk of various colors, in imitation, probably, of the bashaw's *tigue,* or tails. And two ride on each side of him, called *meestrumha dundelmah,* carrying immense spears, with which they are supposed to defend their sultan in action, whose dignity would be infringed upon by defending himself. But the spears are so hung round with charms, and the bearers so abominably unwieldly, that the idea of such weapons being of any use in the hands of such warriors is absurd. Indeed the grotesque appearance of the whole of this prince's train, with heads hung round with charms, and resembling the size and shape of a hogshead—their protruding stomachs and wadded doublets—is ridiculous in the extreme.

The Shaikh of Bornu Reviews His Troops

The sun had scarcely risen this morning when the shaikh was on horseback inspecting his favorite troops, the Kanembu infantry. A hollow space under some sandhills, called Gornamaree, was chosen, about a quarter of a mile from the camp, and the whole was conducted with a good deal of order and system. He was attended to the ground by the four sultans who accompanied the expedition under his orders, and a circle was formed by the Arabs and the Bornu horse. The Shaikh's principal slaves and commanders were dispensed in different parts, habited in their scarlet burnooses with gold lace, and surrounded also by their followers. His own dress was, as usual, neat and simple. Two white figured muslin *tobes,* very large, with a burnoose of the same color, and a cashmere shawl for a turban, composed his dress. Over the whole, across his shoulders, hung the sword which, as he repeatedly said, "The Sultan Inglese had sent him." He was mounted on a very beautiful bright bay horse from Mandara, and took his station on the right side of the circle; while the Kanembus were drawn up on the opposite extremity in close column, to the number of nine thousand. On the signal being made for them to advance, they uttered a yell, or shriek, exceeding anything in shrillness I ever heard; then advanced, by tribes of from eight hundred to one thousand each. They were perfectly naked, with the exception of a rather fantastical belt of the goat or sheepskin, with the hair outward, round their middles, and a few *gubkas* (narrow strips of cloth, the money of the country) round their heads, and brought under the nose. Their arms are a spear and a shield, with a dagger on the left arm reversed, secured by a ring which goes on the wrist, the point running up the arm, and the handle downward. The shields are made of the wood of the fogo, a tree which grows in the shallow waters of the great lake, and are so extremely light as to weigh only a few pounds. The pieces of wood of which it is formed are bound together by thongs of the hides of bullocks with the hair on, which is also carried along the edge of the outside of the shield in vandykes, and forms an ornament. They are something the shape of a gothic window, and most of them slightly convex. Under cover of these, the Kanembu attack the bowmen with great order, and at a slow pace. Their leaders are mounted, and are distinguished merely by a *tobe* of dark blue, and a turban of the same color.

On nearing the spot where the shaikh had placed himself, they quickened their pace, and, after striking their spears against their shields for some seconds, which had an extremely grand and stunning effect, they filed off to the outside of the circle, where they again formed, and awaited their companions, who succeeded them in the same order. There appeared to be a great deal of affection between these troops and the shaikh. He spurred his horse onward into the midst of some tribes as they came up, and spoke to them, while the men crowded round him, kissing his feet, and the stirrups of his saddle. It was a most pleasing sight. He seemed to feel how much his present elevation was owing to their exertions, while they displayed a devotion and attachment deserving and denoting the greatest confidence. I confess I was considerably disappointed at not seeing these troops engage, though more than compensated by the reflection of the slaughter that had been prevented by that disappointment.

8 / THE COMING OF BRASS-CASTING TO BENIN

The forest kingdoms of Benin and Oyo in the southwest part of Nigeria appear to have been founded in the thirteenth century by emigrants from Hausa country, possibly the pagan hard-core who preferred to leave rather than submit to Islam. They settled down as minorities ruling over the native forest peoples—in the case of Benin, the Edos. Jacob Egharevba, who founded his History of Benin *on oral sources, is himself a Benin chief. The passing of the techniques of brass-casting from Ife to Benin in the thirteenth century is one of the all-too-rare recorded details in the history of the two great schools of Nigerian sculpture.*

Oguola, Oba of Benin from about 1280

Obuobo was the eldest son of Ewedo, and was a warlike prince. During his lifetime he led an expedition to Ibo-land, where he remained many years fighting. When he could not be found to be asked to return home, Oguola, the second son of Ewedo, was placed on the throne of Benin after the death and funeral obsequies of his father. Prince Obuobo returned to Benin City three years later, and was therefore made the *ogie* (chief) of Avbiama. The previous titled chiefs of the Ogisos[1] before his arrival there became his own chiefs.

Immediately after his succession, Oguola set men to the great task of digging trenches right round the city to keep out enemies, especially his greatest and most powerful enemy, Akpanigiakon of Udo. This work took over three years. . . .

Soon after this, in order to have peace and liberty, Oguola married one of his daughters to Akpanigiakon. But the princess did not like the idea of the marriage and returned to Benin City from Unuame on the way to Udo, upon which Akpanigiakon declared war against Benin. An expedition headed by Ogiobo was sent to challenge the tyrant and destroy his town. Akpanigiakon was killed at Urhoezien, and the elders of Udo were brought to Benin City where they were executed. The crown of Akpanigiakon was awarded to Ogiobo by the Oba in token of his victory.

Oba Oguola wished to introduce brass-casting into Benin similar to various works of art sent him from Ife. He therefore sent to the Oni of Ife for a brass-smith and Igue-igha was sent to him. Igue-igha was very clever and left many designs to his successors and was in consequence deified and is worshipped to this day by brass-smiths. The practice of making brass castings for the preservation of the records of events was originated during the reign of Oguola. He lived to a very old age.

From Jacob U. Egharevba, *A Short History of Benin* (Benin, 1953), pp. 11, 12. Reprinted by permission of the author.

[1] Before there were Obas in Benin there was a dynasty of kings whose title was Ogiso.

9 / FUNERAL OF A YORUBA KING

The Yorubas are an important group of three million people with common customs and a common language, who inhabit the forest regions of western Nigeria. They were originally all part of the empire of Oyo,[1] which disintegrated during the nineteenth century.

The history of the Yorubas was written by the Reverend Samuel Johnson, a native Yoruba clergyman who lived in the late nineteenth and early twentieth centuries.

The kings are buried in the *bara*. The funeral usually takes place at night. It is notified to the public by the sounding of the *okinkin* (a musical instrument like the bugle), the ivory trumpet and the *koso* drum, a drum which is usually beaten every morning at 4 A.M. as a signal for him to rise from his bed. To beat it at night, therefore, is to indicate that he is retiring to his final resting-place.

The body is removed to the *bara* on the back of those whose office it is to bury the kings, the chief of whom is a titled personage, known as the *ona-onse-awo,* and his lieutenants. At certain stations on the route between the palace and the *bara,* eleven in all, they halt and immolate a man and a ram, and also at the *bara* itself. Four women each at the head and at the feet, two boys at the right and on the left, were usually buried in the same grave with the dead monarch to be his attendants in the other world, and last of all the lamp-bearer in whose presence all the ceremonies are performed.

All these practices, however, have long been abolished, a horse and a bullock being used instead of human beings.

The king is buried in black and white dress; but the crown on his head, the gorgeous robe with which he was laid out in state, and with which his corpse was decked to the *bara,* and the bracelets on his wrists and ankles are never buried with him, these become the perquisites of the *ona-onse-awo* and his lieutenants.

The *bara* in which the kings are buried is distinguished by its aloof situation from public thoroughfares in the outskirts of the city, and having to it as many *kobis* as there are kings lying there,

From Samuel Johnson, *The History of the Yorubas* (London, 1921; Lagos, 1956), pp. 54-57. Reprinted by permission of the C. M. S. (Nigeria) Bookshops.

[1] See extract 8.

one being erected over each. The present *bara* enshrines the bones of King Oluewu, the last of ancient Oyo, with those of the late kings of the present city. It is not open to the public. Several of the late kings' wives are secluded here (as in a convent) and charged with the sole duty of taking care of the graves of their departed husbands.

Their mother superintendent is the *iyamode*, generally styled *Baba* (father). She is thus styled because, being entirely devoted to the worship of Sango, one of the earliest deified kings, she is often "inspired" or "possessed" by the god, and thus came to be regarded as the embodiment of that famous king.

Additions are made to their number at every fresh burial, usually from among the favorites of the deceased husband. These women must all be celibates for life; unfortunately, among the number are usually found some who are virgins and must remain so for life. Any misbehavior is punished with the death of both culprits—the man on the day the crime is detected, and the woman after her confinement.

Besides those who are immolated at the death of the sovereign, there used to be some "honorable suicides" consisting of certain members of the royal family, and some of the king's wives, and others whose title implies that they are to die with the king whenever that event occurs. With the title they received, as a badge, a cloth known as the "death-cloth," a beautiful silk damask wrapper, which they usually arrayed themselves with on special occasions during the king's lifetime. Although the significance of this was well-understood both by themselves and by their relatives, yet it is surprising to see how eager some of them used to be to obtain the office with the title and the cloth. They enjoyed great privileges during the king's lifetime. They can commit any crime with impunity. Criminals condemned to death and escaping to their houses become free. They are never immolated, they are to die honorably and voluntarily.

Of the members of the royal family and others to die were:

1. The *aremo* or crown prince who practically reigned with his father, enjoyed royal honors, and had equal power of life and death.
2. Three princes with hereditary titles, viz. the *Magaji Iyajin*, the *Angunpopo*, and the *Olusami*.

3. Two titled personages not of royal blood, viz. the *Osi-wefa* and the *Olokun-esin* (master of the horse) who is generally styled "Ab obaku," i.e. one who is to die with the king.

4. The female victims were:—

Iya Oba, the king's official mother; Iya Naso, Iyalagbon (the crown prince's mother); Iyale Mole (the Ifa priestess), the *olorun-kumefun,* the *iyamonari,* the *iya-le-ori* (these are all priestesses), and the *are-ori-ite,* the chief favorite.

It will be observed that all the above-mentioned are those who, by virtue of their office, are nearest to the king at all times, and have the easiest access to his person. To make their life dependent on his, therefore, is to ensure safety for him against the risk of poisoning, or the dagger of an assassin.

The custom is that each should go and die in his (or her) own home, and among his family. The spectacle is very affecting. Dressed in their "death-cloth," they issue from the palace to their homes surrounded by their friends, and their drummers beating funeral dirges, eager crowds of friends and acquaintances flocking round them, pressing near to have a last look at them or to say the final farewell as they march homeward. The house is full of visitors, mourners and others, some in profuse tears; mournful dirges and funeral odes are heard on all sides, enough to break the stoutest heart. While the grave is digging, the coffin making, a parting feast is made for all the friends and acquaintances. And as they must die before sunset, they enjoy themselves as best they can for that day by partaking of the choicest and favorite dishes, appearing several times in changes of apparel, distributing presents with a lavish hand around, and making their last will disposing of their effects. When everything is ready, the grave and the coffin approved of, they then take poison, and pass off quietly. But if it fails or is too slow to take effect, and the sun is about to set, the last office is performed by the nearest relatives (by strangling or otherwise) to save themselves and the memory of their kin from indelible disgrace. The body is then decently buried by the relatives and the funeral obsequies performed.

In many cases voluntary suicides take place. Some of the king's favorite slaves who are not required to die often commit suicide in order to attend their master in the other world, expecting to enjoy equally the emoluments of royalty in the other world as in this.

10 / A YORUBA PANTOMIME

On Captain Hugh Clapperton's first expedition to Africa,[1] he came within two hundred miles of the Niger at Sokoto, which he reached in 1824. At the time the mystery of the course and termination of the Niger was still unsolved. He was told at Sokoto that its course was mainly southerly from that point, and that it terminated in the Gulf of Guinea. When he returned to England with this information, the British government sent him out on a further expedition with the object of reaching the river from the Guinea coast. The description of the Yoruba pantomime is taken from his journal of this second expedition, brought home, after his death at Sokoto, by his servant John Lander. The performance was given at Old Oyo, the capital of the principal Yoruba kingdom.

It is the custom, during the time that the *caboceers*[2] from the different towns remain on their visit to the king, to act plays or pantomimes, or whatever they may be called. I shall attempt a description of the one I saw today. The place chosen for this pastime is the king's park, fronting the principal door where his majesty usually sits. A fetish house occupies the left side; to the south are two very romantic and large blocks of granite, by the side of which is an old withered tree. On the east are some beautiful shady trees; and on the north his majesty's house, from whence he views the scene. In the center are two beautiful clumps of trees; in one of which is a tall fan-palm, overlooking the whole area, a space that may include some seven or eight hundred yards square. Under these clumps of trees were seated the actors, dressed in large sacks, covering every part of the body; the head most fantastically decorated with strips of rags—damask, silk, and cotton of as many glaring colors as it was possible. The king's servants attended to keep the peace, and to prevent the crowd from breaking into the square in which the actors were assembled. Musicians also attended with drums, horns, and whistles, which were beaten and blown without intermission.

The first act consisted in dancing and tumbling in sacks, which

From Hugh Clapperton, *Journal of a Second Expedition into the Interior of Africa* (London, 1829), pp. 53-56.

[1] See extract 7.
[2] Officials or chiefs.

they performed to admiration, considering they could not see, and had not the free use of their feet and hands. The second act consisted in catching the *boa-constrictor*. First, one of the sack-men came in front and knelt down on his hands and feet; then came out a tall majestic figure, having on a headdress and mask which baffle all description. It was of a glossy black color, sometimes like a lion couchant over the crest of a helmet; at another like a black head with a large wig. At every turn he made, it changed its appearance. This figure held in its right hand a sword, and by its superior dress and motions appeared to be the director of the scene, for not a word was spoken by the actors. The manager, as I shall call the tall figure, then came up to the man who was lying in the sack; another sack-dancer was brought in his sack, who by a wave of the sword was laid down at the other's head or feet; he, having unsewn the end of both sacks, the two crawled into one. There was now great waving of the manager's sword. Indeed I thought that heads were going to be taken off, as all the actors were assembled round the party lying down. But in a few minutes they all cleared away, except the manager, who gave two or three flourishes with his sword, when the representation of the boa-constrictor began. The animal put its head out of the bag in which it was contained, attempting to bite the manager; but at a wave of the sword it threw its head in another direction to avert the blow. It then began gradually to creep out of the bag, and went through the motions of a snake in a very natural manner, though it appeared to be rather full in the belly; opening and shutting its mouth, which I suspect was the performer's two hands, in the most natural manner imaginable. The length of the creature was spun out to fourteen feet; and the color and action were well represented by a covering of painted cloth, imitating that of the boa. After following the manager round the park for some time, and attempting to bite him, which he averted by a wave of the sword, a sign was made for the body of actors to come up; when the manager, approaching the tail, made flourishes with his sword as if hacking in that part of the body. The snake gasped, twisted up, and seemed as if in great torture; and when nearly dead, it was shouldered by the masked actors, still gasping and making attempts to bite, but was carried off in triumph to the fetish house.

The third act consisted of the white devil. The actors having retired to some distance in the background, one of them was left in the center, whose sack falling gradually down, exposed a white head, at which all the crowd gave a shout that rent the air. They appeared indeed to enjoy this sight, as the perfection of the actor's art. The whole body was at last cleared of the encumbrance of the sack, when it exhibited the appearance of a human figure cast in white wax, of the middle size, miserably thin, and starved with cold. It frequently went through the motion of taking snuff and rubbing its hands. When it walked, it was with the most awkward gait, treading as the most tender-footed white man would do in walking barefooted, for the first time, over new-frozen ground. The spectators often appealed to us, as to the excellence of the performance, and entreated I would look and be attentive to what was going on. I pretended to be fully as much pleased with this caricature of a white man as they could be, and certainly the actor burlesqued the part to admiration. This being concluded, the performers all retired to the fetish house. Between each act, we had choral songs by the king's women, in which the assembled crowd joined their voices.

11 / THE EIGHTEENTH-CENTURY EXPANSION OF DAHOMEY, AND THE ORIGIN OF THE WOMEN'S ARMY

The following extracts, from A History of Dahomey *compiled by Archibald Dalzel, contain accounts of the expansion of the kingdom of Dahomey to the coast in the 1720s, and, incidentally, of the founding of the famous women's army of Dahomey. Dalzel, who spent thirty years in Africa, was for four years governor of the British fort at Whydah, and subsequently governor at Cape Coast. His book was compiled from notes supplied by Lionel Abson, his successor at Whydah, and from the already considerable travel literature on Dahomey. His principal source for the events described here was Captain Snelgrave, who had been in Whydah at the time. It should be noted that the women's army became a regular part of the Dahomey fighting force. The ruling house of Dahomey was probably an off-shoot of that of Yoruba and Benin.*

At this time Whydah was governed by a weak and indolent prince,

From Archibald Dalzel, *A History of Dahomey* (London, 1793), pp. 16-20, 55, 56.

who, having ascended the throne at the age of fourteen, soon became the tool of a train of designing ministers. They flattered his natural disposition for dissipation and effeminacy, as the surest means of sharing his power; and now at the age of thirty, he was neither qualified for the council nor the field. His indolence and indulgence had swollen him to an enormous size; and, constantly shut up in his seraglio, amongst thousands of women, over whom he asserted the most despotic sway, he vainly imagined his bulk to be the type of his real greatness. Meanwhile the ministers and *caboceers* around him, intent on their own private interests, divided the state into a thousand different factions, which, added to the natural timidity of the people, the result of plenty, long ease, and inaction, exposed it as a ready prey to any invader.

When threatened with the Dahoman invasion, this vain creature made so light of both the people and their king, that, though it is the constant custom of these nations to destroy princes and great men taken in war, lest their power and knowledge should excite the conquered nation to rebellion; yet, in bravado, he told Snelgrave, he would not even cut off the king of Dahomey's head, when taken; but would keep him alive as a slave in one of the most contemptible situations about his person. This foolish speech, which, no doubt, reached the ears of Trudo, probably helped to exasperate him. Accordingly, when he had made the necessary preparations, he first attacked the northern part of the kingdom, which was under the hereditary government of a great lord, then called Appragah, who forthwith sent to the king of Whydah for assistance; but, through the interest of his enemies at court, was, most strangely, refused. Whereupon, after a slight resistance, Appragah submitted to and was kindly received by the king of Dahomey, who afterward reinstated him in his possessions.

The conqueror immediately prepared to penetrate into the heart of the country. For which purpose he encamped on the banks of a river that runs about half a mile to the northward of Sabee or Xavier, the capital of Whydah. Here he expected a vigorous opposition; for, having neither boats nor boatmen, his army could only pass the river by fording; and even this was not practicable, except at one place, which five hundred resolute men could easily have defended against the efforts of his whole army. But he was deceived; for instead of using the necessary precaution to prevent the incursions of so dreadful an enemy, the Whydahs left the pass to the care of the Snake, their Fetish or god, to whom they sacrificed night and morning, praying him to prevent the enemy from crossing the river. And satisfied with this, they even omitted, which is scarcely credible, to keep so much as a guard there.

Trudo, probably supposing his whole force might be necessary for this enterprise, had left the conduct of this part of his army to his general, and was gone to bring down the other part, which was encamped at his headquarters at Ardra; having first sent an intimation to the European factors, as he had formerly done to those at Ardra, that he expected them to remain neutral, under pain of his resentment. The general, observing the enemy's neglect, ordered 200 men to try the ford; which having done unmolested, they, being resolute fellows, immediately proceeded on to the town, without waiting for further orders, shouting and sounding their war music all the way. This happening about three o'clock in the afternoon, the out-guards of the town were almost all fast asleep; but being wakened by the noise, they fled into the town, crying out that all the Dahoman army had passed the river. This no sooner was announced, than king and people began to decamp; and in a very short time the fields were covered with men, women, and children, flying from all parts towards the seaside. The king and many of his train, by the help of canoes, got safe to the islands near Popo; but numbers who could not obtain that conveyance were, in their hurry, drowned in attempting to swim over to them. Those slain and made prisoners were innumerable; and thousands, who sheltered themselves up and down the country among the bushes, afterward perished by sword and famine.

The Dahoman general could not believe the reports that were brought to him of his good fortune; nor scarce trust to the evidence of his own senses, when, having conducted over the remainder of his army, which he did the same evening, he saw the truth confirmed: "that two hundred soldiers had put to flight a nation capable of opposing them with a thousand men to one." So wretched a creature is man, when enervated by luxury, indolence, and servile passions!

There is no other way of accounting for this imbecility of mind, this panic fear with which so great a nation must have been struck, on such a trifling alarm. Though they pretended afterwards, when some of those who had escaped were upbraided with the cowardly manner in which they had deserted their country, that it was "for fear of being eaten; that the Dahomans were cannibals, whom nothing could resist; and that the thought of being devoured by their own species, was far more terrible to them than their apprehension about being killed."

[*The king of Whydah and his followers took refuge on an island. King Trudo gave the Whydahs permission to return to their country on the condition that they hand their king over to him, but they refused to do this. With the help of a gallant captain from the islands called Ossue, they made one unsuccessful attempt to return by force. They then sent word of their distress to the king of Oyo, a traditional enemy of Dahomey. In 1728 a large Oyo army was amassed to invade Dahomey. This met with great success, and the Dahomans retreated, pursuing a "scorched earth" policy. When the Whydahs heard that the Dahomans were in dire straits, and forced to eat their slaves, they took advantage of an invitation from the governor of the British fort at Whydah to stage a successful return, having first acquired the Popos as allies. In the meantime the rains had forced the invading Oyos to retire, and Trudo set to work to rebuild his kingdom. He despatched a party of slaves under escort to the coast, to be exchanged for trade goods. His emissaries found that the Whydahs barred the way.*]

Amazed at this, they quickly returned, and informed their master of what they had seen. The king was struck with the news. The number of his soldiers had been greatly reduced by the Oyos; he had lately sent an army against some of the inland countries; so that he might have reasonably been excused, had he considered his remaining troops as insufficient to attack the combined force of Whydah and Popo. But Trudo, equally politic as brave, and who had before experienced the timidity of one part of his enemies, thought the very appearance of number would be sufficient to put them to flight; the other he knew he was still more than able to cope withal. He thereupon speedily collected together his remaining troops, forming with them the vanguard of the army. The rear he composed of a great number of women, armed like soldiers, having their proper officers, and furnished like regular troops, with drums, colors, and umbrellas, making at a distance a very formidable appearance. With these he marched against the combined armies who, surprised at the appearance of such a force when they expected the Dahomans were quite reduced, began to debate on the propriety of a retreat. Ossue and the Popos determined to stand their ground, and the king encouraged his part to do the like. The battle began. Ossue and the Popo general attacked the Dahoman right wing with so much vigor that they drove them for some time before them; but the troops under the Whydah king gave way at the first onset, and fled, notwithstanding all the efforts of their leader, who wounded several of them with his lance in their flight. The Dahomans, feeling this, rallied; and, in their turn, attacking the rear of the Ossue's troops, put them and the Popos to the rout.

12 / THE ANNUAL "KING'S CUSTOMS" OF DAHOMEY

There are many good English descriptions of the notorious annual "Customs" of Dahomey, several of which date from the eighteenth century. The nineteenth-century account by Sir Richard Burton, the great traveler who visited King Gelele of Dahomey at the end of 1863 and the beginning of 1864, was chosen because of the vividness of his narrative.

Although many details of the "Customs" give evidence of considerable contact with European trade, the ritual is basically West African and only superficially influenced by outside contact. Several of the other powerful West African kingdoms had similar rituals. The annual "Customs" were a continuation of the more prolonged and elaborate—and more bloodthirsty—"Grand Customs" which took place on a king's succession. They were of two kinds. The first was called "Atto-ton-khwe," or "Atto year"—from the "Atto," or platform, from which the human sacrificial victims were thrown, trussed, to the waiting swordsmen below. The second, called "So-sin-khwe," or "Horse-tie year," was witnessed by Burton, and his description is the only account of this form of the "Customs." The number of human victims, which varied from king to king, has often been greatly exaggerated. Burton did not witness the actual killing, as his predecessors had done—possibly because of the nature of his mission, which was to persuade Gelele to abandon the whole thing.

Although his vivid description is sometimes marred by jeering, he was nonetheless able to understand the strong religious feeling underlying the sacrificial ritual. He says, in one of several appeals

*for an understanding of it: "It is no mere delight in torture and
death which underlies the rite in these lands. The king has to perform a disagreeable task over his ancestral graves, and he does it.
His subjects would deem it impious were he to curtail or to omit
the performance, and suddenly to suppress it would be as if a
European monarch were forcibly to abolish prayers for the dead."* [1]

The "So-sin-khwe Customs" of Dahomey

The First Day

Early on the Day of the Innocents (December 28th 1863), a dis-
charge of musketry near the palace and a royal message informed
us that the Customs had begun, and that our presence at the palace
was expected. We delayed as long as was decent, and, shortly after
noon, mounting our hammocks, we proceeded by the usual way
to the Kumasi House.

In the Uhun-jro marketplace, outside the Ako-chyo Gate, and
not attached, as it used to be, to the palace wall, stood a victim
shed, completed and furnished. From afar the shape was not unlike
that of an English village church—a barn and a tower. The total
length was about one hundred feet, the breadth forty, and the
greatest height sixty. It was made of roughly squared posts, nine
feet high, and planted deep in the earth. The ground floor of the
southern front had sixteen poles, upon which rested the joists and
planks supporting the pent-shaped roof of the barn. There was a
western double storied turret, each front having four posts. The
whole roof was covered with a tattered cloth, blood red, bisected
by a single broad stripe of blue check.

In the turret and in the barn were twenty victims. All were
seated on cage stools, and were bound to the posts which passed
between their legs; the ankles, the shins under the knees, and the
wrists being lashed outside with connected ties. Necklaces of rope,
passing behind the back, and fastened to the upper arms, were also
made tight to the posts. The confinement was not cruel: each victim
had an attendant squatting behind him, to keep off the flies; all

From Richard Burton, *A Mission to King Gelele of Dahomey* (London, 1893),
Vol. I, pp. 232-56; Vol. II, pp. 1-41.

[1] P. 117.

were fed four times a day, and were loosed at night for sleep. As will be shown, it is the king's object to keep them in the best of humors.

The dress of these victims was that of state criminals. They wore long white nightcaps, with spirals of blue ribbon sewn on, and calico shirts of *quasi*-European cut, decorated round the neck and down the sleeves with red bindings, and with a crimson patch on the left breast. The remaining garment was a loincloth, almost hidden by the "camise." It was an ominous sight; but at times the king exposes without slaying his victims. A European under the circumstances would have attempted to escape, and in all probability would have succeeded. These men will allow themselves to be led to the slaughter like lambs. It is, I imagine, the uncertainty of their fate that produces the extraordinary *nonchalance*. They marked time to music, and they chattered together, especially remarking us. Possibly they were speculating upon the chances of a pardon.

We dismounted, as usual, at the palace corner, and the Harmattan sun made us take refuge under one of the sheds. A procession was walking round the square—a mob of followers escorting the *sogan,* or horse captain, who was riding bareheaded under a white umbrella. This high official who is under the meu,[1] opens the Customs by taking all the chargers from their owners, and by tying them up, whence the word "So-sin." The animals must be redeemed after a few days, with a bag of cowries. A gun, fired inside the palace, warned us that royalty was about to appear. A corps of "Amazons" [2] streamed from, and formed a rough line in front of, the Kumasi Gate. The king, under a gorgeous umbrella and the usual parasol upheld by his wives, stalked down a lane through the thick crowd toward his own proper So-sin. This was a shanty fronting, and about 150 paces from, the palace. It resembled the Uhunjro, or market shed to the north-northeast, but it lacked the turret. Thirty barked and badly dressed tree trunks and a strong scantling of roughly squared timber supported the first floor, which was without walls. The thatch of the pent-roof was hidden, as in the other So-sin, by a glaring blood red calico, with long black stripes along

---

[1] The second minister of state.
[2] The European name for the famous women's army of Dahomey. (See extract 11.)

the ridge and eaves. Splints of bamboo frond were planted in the ground, and a thin cord of "tie-tie," [3] or tree bark, railed off between them and the public a space, some four feet broad, into which only the king is allowed to penetrate. I counted nine victims on the ground floor and ten above, lashed to nearly every second post of the front opposite the palace. They resembled in all points those of the market shed, and looked wholly unconcerned, whilst their appearance did not attract the least attention. Yet I felt haunted by the presence of these *morituri,* with whose hard fate the dance, the song, the dole, and the noisy merriment of the thoughtless mob afforded the saddest contrast.

Between the Kumasi Gate and this "palace shed" was planted a tall T-shaped pole, rough, black, and hung with white rugs at each end of the crosspiece. This is a Bo fetish, guarding the present Custom. Near it, under a pair of exceedingly shabby umbrellas, sat, on the dignity of *caboceers'* [4] chairs and stools, the representatives of the Agasun-no, the highest fetisheer in the city. The head man, or deputy, wore a huge flapped felt hat, and a body-cloth striped blue and white. When the Agasun-no appears in person before the monarch the latter must remove his sandals, prostrate himself before the church, kiss the ground, and throw a little dust upon his forehead, whilst all the courtiers take a sand bath, and white men stand up and bow. Methought they did not regard us with an overfriendly eye, but such is, perhaps, the custom of reverend men generally with respect to those not of their own persuasion.

The king, having visited his fetish, returned toward the palace, surrounded by five of his principal officers. At a signal we advanced, bared heads, shook hands, and snapped fingers with him; he cordially and repeatedly returned the compliment, inquiring politely about our health. He then returned to his station near the palace gate, where the Amazons, after sallying out and parading about the square amongst the prostrate men, returned to him. The royal shed was ostentatiously small, open, and covered with poor colored cloths: a line of twelve umbrellas, the two most gorgeous being outside, formed a verandah, and inside the parasol showed the place of the king. He occupied a kind of couch, strewed with handsome homemade cottons; in front of him, upon a mat,

[3] Pidgin English for string.
[4] Officials.

crouched a *dakro,* or messengeress, and behind him stood and sat a semicircle of wives. On the king's proper right was a larger shed, somewhat like a two poled tent. The mat and thatch were covered with cloth, parti-colored at the sides and at the roof, whilst elsewhere it was of white calico, adorned with grotesque shapes. Unlike its neighbor, it was closed all round except at the entrance, which had for verandah two white umbrellas. Inside, at the bottom, was a kind of divan, and on the ground before it sat a small black child in red, and two women with white caps and vests, and blue pagnes, with four or five others hardly distinguishable. The double posts supporting the entrance were clothed with red and pink silk; about their middle hung a dozen abacot caps, and under the verandah squatted a woman with a gun placed on a stool before her.

The tent contained the relics of the old king. His ghost is supposed to be present, and all bow and prostrate to it before noticing the present ruler.

To Gelele's extreme right was planted a white flag, with a blue cross; around the staff a group of armed women gathered. Immediately near the king, but leaving a spare space in front, were the Amazons, at squat, with their gun barrels bristling upwards. There were amongst them many young girls in training for military life. A half naked boy lay on the ground within a few feet of the royal umbrellas, and children are allowed behind the bamboos. On other occasions, juveniles, wholly nude, wandered about, heedless of reproof, and I have seen two of them fighting before the throne. Even the lowest orders crossed the presence with an air for which, in Asia, their feet and calves would have disappeared under the bastinado. . . .

On the left of the king were the Amazon drums and rattles. In the open space between the throne and the bamboos lay the three calabashes supporting the three chieftains' brass mounted skulls. On two large mats of palm fiber were ranged shallow baskets, which acted as saucers to calabashes some 2.5 feet in diameter. Three of them were adorned with silver crescents and stars, whilst all were covered above and below with various colored calicoes— red, blue, yellow, pink, and striped. Periodically, knots of eight or nine women came from the palace with larger or smaller gourds of provisions, which they disposed upon a third mat in front of the king.

In a much shorter time than it has taken the reader to peruse the *mise en scène*, the *caboceers* and their followers, who were scattered over the square, gathered into a dense semicircle near the bamboos. The dignitaries sat or lay on the ground, unarmed, under their white, blue, and fancy umbrellas. The little people were on foot behind them, and the women and girls stood aloof, peeping as best they could. The total number present, including about 300 children, might have amounted to 2500, and I never saw at Abomey a larger gathering.

[*Having painted the scene, Burton describes various preliminary happenings, including a "sally of the Amazons" to the accompaniment of long and loud firing. Then the chief actor takes the stage again.*]

Gelele then rose, and came from out his shed. His dress, besides the usual *braccae* and a dark silk kerchief round his waist, was a blue-flowered damask shirt, a table-cover, in fact, and this was knotted on the left side. He formed an effective picture; a fine tall figure, with shoulders towering above his wives, the head bent slightly forwards, and his hands clasped behind his back. There were hushed murmurs of applause, and the faces of his subjects expressed unaffected admiration.

The king having hitched up his body-cloth, began an allocution in a low tone, as if nervous. Men and women *huissiers* and heralds, standing on the right, and the youths calling themselves the "Donpwe," proclaimed attention by loud and long cries of "Ago!" Audience!—or "Oyez!" On the left a sharp double tap was struck on the cymbal, and all obeyed. The king spoke with the head a little on one side, assuming a somewhat *goguenard* air. His words were many and oft repeated; the genius, or rather the poverty, of the language necessitates verbosity. In so artless a tongue it is only by "battology" and frequent repetition that the finer shades of meaning can be elicited. The sense is short to relate. His ancestors had built rough and simple So-sin sheds. His father Gezo had improved them when "making Customs" for the ghost of Agongoro (Wheenoohew).[5] It is good to beget children who can perform such pious rites. Therefore, he (Gelele) would do for his sire what he hoped

---

[5] Gelele's grandfather.

his son would do for him. And some score of men sat listening—about to die!

Presently the women in attendance placed the drums before the king, and handed to him four hooked sticks. Upon these he spat, beat two of the instruments, and spoke during the intervals of drumming. The "Ganchya," I was told, is a new ceremony.

After listening to loud applause, and being saluted with discharges of musketry, the king retired behind the curtain held by his wives, and whilst he drank, the subjects went through the usual ceremony.

After resting awhile, Gelele stalked to the fore. In his left hand was a *kpo-ge,* or singer's staff, a silver-headed and ferruled stick, two feet long. To the upper part was fastened a square of silk kerchief, striped red and purple, and folded in a triangle. The apex was passed through silver-lined eyelet holes, like those that in former times, amongst us, held the "beau's" cane tassel. The king also wore the bard's insignia, double necklaces of beads, disposed like cross belts over the breast, and with the usual pigtails behind. After singing for a while, to the great delight of the listeners, he danced, first to the men's, then to the women's, band. He is, unlike his father, a notable performer, and though his style is purely Dahoman and barbarous, the movements are comparatively kingly and dignified. He was assisted in this performance by a "leopard wife" [6] on each side, dressed in white waistcoats, and striped loincloths extending to the feet. In their hair was a kind of diadem of silver pieces, bright as new sixpences. At this sight the people vociferated their joy. A herald, in a huge felt hat and bright bracelets, and a jester, conspicuously ugly, with a tattered "wide-awake," a large goatskin bag under the left arm, with chalked faces and legs, rose to their feet, and pointing at the king—a peculiarly disrespectful action to European eyes—declared, in cracked, shouting voices, that he was "Sweet, sweet, sweet as a white man!" Then followed a chorus of soldier-esses, and from the crowd loud "Ububu," made by patting the open mouth with the hand. On the women's side the "king's birds" chirruped and twittered to justify their names.

Before sitting down, Gelele advanced to the front rank of male spectators, and, removing with his right forefinger the perspiration from his brow, scattered it with a jerk over the delighted group.

[6] The leopard wives were the youngest and the fairest of the harem.

He was then cooled by his wives, who rubbed him down with fine yellow silk kerchiefs, and vigorously plied their round hide fans, colored and embroidered.

Then, rising again, like a refreshed giant, the monarch danced to six modes. When the time was to be changed, a chorus of women gave the cue to their band by repeating certain meaningless technical terms, ending with frequent repetitions of "Ko! ko! ko!" till the musician had learned the right measure. Presently, two, and at a short interval, three wives danced on each side of the king, keeping an eye upon him, and so preserving excellent time. The fourth dance was more animated, and as the monarch showed shortage of breath, an old Amazon addressed him, "Adan-we!" [7] He resumed his labors to the words, "Agida hun-to Ko-hun!" [8] and he advanced, stooping towards the ground, and rolling one elbow over another, to show that he was binding captives.

Followed a little change of scene. The king, propping his elbow upon the bard's staff, and bending low whilst his wives surrounded him, sitting on their hams, sang, and was responded to by what appeared a laughing chorus, but which was a dirge, a single cymbal making melancholy music. Then rising with uplifted staff, and turning towards the larger shed-tent, he adored, in silence, his father's ghost. This new and startling practice was twice repeated.

The rest of the first day of the Customs was taken up with such things as the distribution of decorations, and the ritual connected with new appointments to high office. Burton's party was tactfully let off with only slight participation in the dancing. After the arrival of the provisions, they withdrew to their lodging, from where they heard the noises of feasting all night. The second day of the Customs, known as the "Avo uzu gbe," or cloth-changing day, was postponed for twenty-four hours because of the indisposition of Burton and his party. Gelele, dressed in a number of different costumes, executed some very intricate dance movements in full view of the audience. A patchwork cloth over a thousand feet long, which was to be worn by the reigning monarch in the event of the defeat of Abeokuta[9] was displayed. For the rest of the day the processions circled unendingly, as on the first day.

[7] "Oh brave white!"
[8] "Drummer, use thy drum-stick, and we will turn about."
[9] The city state of Abeokuta was a traditional enemy of Dahomey.

The Third Day

[*The events of the third day began at three-thirty in the afternoon. Ministers, ministresses, hunchbacks with dwarf fetishes, chiefs with their private escorts of Amazons, passed, or stayed to caper before the throne. The principal event of the day was the distribution of, and scramble for, cowry shells.*]

The king then rose and walked forward to throw cowries, the local money, among his subjects. All removed their ornaments and girt their loins; it is a point of honor to fight for the royal *bakhshish,* and nob and snob join in the melee. No notice is taken if a man be killed or maimed in the affair; he has fallen honorably fighting for his sovereign. . . .

He [the king] took from baskets, which were brought up in turn to him, heads of strung cowries, and tossed them high up to the crowd, who fought for them as if they were gold. The bundles were torn to pieces in a moment, so were the strings, and at times there was a scramble, a bite, and a scream about a single shell. . . .

The king then walked up to the victim shed, and paced down its length within the railing. To the score of wretches there sitting pilloried he threw with two hands many heads of cowries, and these were placed by the attendants upon the caps of the recipients. He conversed freely with several of them. The others, though I could see no sign, were probably gagged, for the reason before stated.[10] He then came and snapped fingers with me, when a hint was given that at my intercession several victims would be pardoned. This also is a Dahoman formula. I pleaded for them, saying that mercy is the great prerogative of kings, when nearly half of them were brought up before Gelele, were untied, and were placed by the keepers on all fours to hear the royal clemency.

The Fourth Day

[*The fourth day was called "So-nan-wen-kan'gbe," which means "horse untie day." Burton, however, does not describe any ceremonial connected with horses. It is possible that the horse ritual had, to some extent, dropped from use. The spectacles of this day had a very military flavor.*]

Adan-men-nun-kon of the guard, supported by a three-deep col-

[10] If a victim spoke to the king he had to be pardoned.

umn of fifty men, stood up, and, in the bawling barking tone affected by the real brave, declared that as the Fanti Company had sung about breaking Abeokuta, so the Blue had sworn to destroy it. The sentiment was seconded by the *gau* and the *matro* with such jumping and breast beating that a stranger would suppose them to be in a violent rage. The general uproar of captains, the dance, and presenting arms—sticks and knives—testified their general joy, and they chanted to the effect that they would not only knock down the walls of Abeokuta, but they would also carry away the bits for Gelele their king. . . .

The women, having re-formed a single peloton five deep, Ji-bi-whe-ton, their colonel-ess, issued from the midst of them. Her scalp was clean-shaven and shining, a single little lock held a silver knob like the finial of a teapot, and her chief ornament was the common *fleur-de-lis* of silver attached by a chain to her neck. She wore a vest, pink before and white behind, with a drooping slovenly collar. A black leather cartridge belt kept in position her long blue-striped waistcloth and confined on her left hip an ammunition bag, whilst her right hand grasped the muzzle of a short musket, to which were hung many charms. In hoarse manly tones she called out severally her best women, each of whom sharply responded "Tamule! O Brave!" presented them to the king, handed to them their cowries, placed the bundles upon their heads, and dismissed them. Some of the more forward made short speeches with a pert air, and struck their bosoms, as to say, "I am the woman to do it, I." At times a dozen or two stood up, sang and raised one or both arms, the forefinger as usual being extended, thus swearing to brave deeds before the king.

Similarly Adan-men-nun-kon presented his chosen warriors, who, unlike the women, prostrated themselves. At one name, Mocho, the captainesses laughed satirically, showing the rivalry ever existing between the two sexes. The women, naturally somewhat incontinent of tongue, also supply all omissions and explanations of the men's speeches, whilst these dare not interrupt their sister soldiers. On the other hand the full private, the jester, the bushman, in fact everyone, addresses his sovereign without interruption, demanding and receiving audience and justice. So far the despotism is quite *en règle:* it is the progressive democratic, not the barbarous aristocratic. Lastly there was a general "Tamule!" The women sang and clapped hands, whilst the elite danced. This example was duly followed by the men.

Silence having been once more proclaimed, the king spoke fiercely about the capture of Abeokuta, and he was seconded by Adan-men-nun-kon the Brave. The women fired, the men blew their horns, and both companies, masculine and feminine, sang to this purport: "We refused to let our king furnish his father's grave with any skulls and bones save those of the Egbas. These we swear now to procure for him. If the foe soar in the air we will fly, if he dive we will follow him, if he sink in earth we will descend after him." The king excitedly informed them that he would see the oath kept. The Blues rushed tumultuously afar, skirmishing and firing. Presently they returned at a *pas de charge,* and clustered before the king, whilst the women chanted Nago songs, in which they are said to excel.

[Intricate maneuvers followed each other almost interminably throughout the long day that preceded the Zan Nyanyana or Evil Night of human sacrifice.]

As we wended our way homeward from the palace to the city gate, we found both sides of the road lined with bamboo railing, to keep the thoroughfare clear for the king. It serves its purpose [as] effectually as policemen and Life Guards in England. Tonight Gelele will walk in procession with his wives, and attended by the high officials, from the Kumasi House to the Uhun-jro market place, where the Mingan will perform sundry executions with his own hand.

As sometimes happens, the subject of *men-huwu* or human sacrifice in Dahomey has been thoroughly misunderstood in the press and the public at home. It is by no means done to "keep up the good old customs of the country." The object is not to "offer a valuable and acceptable present to heaven"; nor is it penance or self-deprivation done because the thing parted with is precious or coveted. The king takes no pleasure in the tortures and death, or in the sight of blood, as will presently appear. . . . Any encyclopedia will show that human sacrifice, like slavery, is almost universally a concomitant of a certain stage of civilization, and that with the increase of knowledge it disappears forever.

Human sacrifice in Dahomey is founded upon a purely religious basis, which not only strengthens but perpetuates the custom. It is a touching instance of the king's filial piety, deplorably mistaken, but perfectly sincere. The Dahoman sovereign must, I have said, enter Deadland with royal state.

The Fifth Day

During the night, at times the deep sound of the death-drum and the loud report of the musket informed us that some mortal spirit had fled. . . . I was debating whether to decline attending at the palace, as desired to do on the "glad day," when, as if the king had divined my intention, the Prince Chyu-da-ton called upon me at an early hour and explained that all those slain during the last evil night were criminals and captives. . . . The approach to the palace was not pleasant. The northeastern or market shed was empty; out of its tenants, nine had perished. Four corpses attired in their criminals' shirts and nightcaps were sitting in pairs on Gold Coast stools, supported by a double storied scaffold, about forty feet high, of rough beams, two perpendiculars and as many connecting horizontals. At a little distance, on a similar erection, but made for half the number, were two victims, one above the other. Between these substantial affairs was a gallows of thin posts, some thirty feet tall, with a single victim hanging by the heels, head downward. Lastly, planted close to the path was a *patibulum* for two, dangling side by side. Fine cords, passed in several coils round the ankles and above the knees, attached them to the crossbar of the gallows, and the limpness of their limbs showed that the "dear breath" had lately been beaten out of them. There were no signs of violence upon the bodies, which were wholly nude: They had been mutilated after death, in respect to the royal wives, and very little blood appeared upon the ground below.

We then passed to the southeastern gate of the Kumasi House, where the palace shed was also untenanted. In front of sundry little black dolls, stuck in the ground at both sides of the entrance, lay a dozen heads. They were in two batches of six each, disposed in double lines of three; their faces were downwards, and the cleanly severed necks caught the observer's eye. Around each heap was raised a rim of white ashes. These victims had probably been slaughtered directly in front of the gate, as there were traces of blood there. The bodies had been removed, so as not to offend the king. Within the palace entrance were two more, making a total of fourteen. Thus, during king's "Evil Night," twenty-three human beings had lost their lives.[11]

13 / RECEPTION OF AN ENGLISH MISSION IN ASHANTI IN 1817

The Mande states, of which ancient Ghana and Mali were the most important, were the ancestors of the forest states of modern Ghana. The most powerful of these, Ashanti, carried out an invading expedition to the coast in 1807. This, and subsequent invasions in 1811 and 1816, laid waste the country of the Fanti and considerably interrupted the trade of the European coastal forts. Both of these facts made an English mission to the king of Ashanti desirable. On April 22nd, 1817 an embassy bound for Kumasi, the capital of Ashanti, left the English castle at Cape Coast. Its objects were to establish peaceful trading relations and to bring back a scientific account of the interior. The party, consisting of Messrs. James, Bowdich, Hutchison, and Tedlie, with a small escort, reached Kumasi on May 19th. They were amazed at the splendor of the Ashanti court, where many of the ornaments were of solid gold.

Our observations *en passant* had taught us to conceive a spectacle far exceeding our original expectations; but they had not prepared us for the extent and display of the scene which here burst upon us. An area of nearly a mile in circumference was crowded with magnificence and novelty. The king, his tributaries, and captains were resplendent in the distance, surrounded by attendants of every description, fronted by a mass of warriors which seemed to make our approach impervious. The sun was reflected, with a glare scarcely more supportable than the heat, from the massy gold ornaments, which glistened in every direction. More than a hundred bands burst at once on our arrival, with the peculiar airs of their

From T. Edward Bowdich, *Mission from Cape Coast to Ashanti* (London, 1819), pp. 34-37.

[11] Burton had reason to believe that some female victims were also done to death by the Amazons behind the scenes.

several chiefs. The horns flourished their defiances, with the beating of innumerable drums and metal instruments, and then yielded for a while to the soft breathings of their long flutes, which were truly harmonious; and a pleasing instrument, like a bagpipe without the drone, was happily blended. At least a hundred large umbrellas, or canopies, which could shelter thirty persons, were sprung up and down by the bearers with brilliant effect, being made of scarlet, yellow, and the most showy cloths and silks, and crowned on the top with crescents, pelicans, elephants, barrels, and arms and swords of gold. . . . The state hammocks, like long cradles, were raised in the rear, the poles on the heads of the bearers. The cushions and pillows were covered with crimson taffeta, and the richest cloths hung over the sides. Innumerable small umbrellas of various colored stripes, were crowded in the intervals, whilst several large trees heightened the glare, by contrasting the sober coloring of nature. . . .

The king's messengers, with gold breastplates, made way for us, and we commenced our round, preceded by the canes[1] and the English flag. We stopped to take the hand of every *caboceer*,[2] which, as their household suites occupied several spaces in advance, delayed us long enough to distinguish some of the ornaments in the general blaze of splendor and ostentation.

The *caboceers,* as did their superior captains and attendants, wore Ashanti cloths[3] of extravagant price from the costly foreign silks which had been unravelled to weave them in all the varieties of color, as well as pattern. They were an incredible size and weight, and thrown over the shoulder exactly like the Roman toga. A small silk fillet generally encircled their temples, and massy gold necklaces, intricately wrought, suspended Moorish[4] charms, dearly purchased, and enclosed in small square cases of gold, silver, and curious embroidery. Some wore necklaces reaching to the navel entirely of *aggry*[5] beads. A band of gold and beads encircled the knee, from which several strings of the same depended. Small circles of gold like guineas, rings, and casts of

[1] The interpreters' symbol.
[2] Officials or chiefs.
[3] Now known as Kenti cloths.
[4] Muslim.
[5] Blue beads common in West Africa.

animals were strung round their ankles. Their sandals were of green, red, and delicate white leather. Manillas[6] and rude lumps of rock gold hung from their left wrists, which were so heavily laden as to be supported on the head of one of their handsomest boys. Gold and silver pipes and canes dazzled the eye in every direction. Wolves and rams heads as large as life, cast in gold, were suspended from their gold-handled swords, which were held round them in great numbers. . . . The king's four linguists were encircled by a splendor inferior to none, and their peculiar insignia, gold canes, were elevated in all directions, tied in bundles like fasces. The keeper of the treasury added to his own magnificence by the ostentatious display of his service; the blow pan, boxes, scales, and weights were of solid gold.

A delay of some minutes whilst we severally approached to receive the king's hand afforded us a thorough view of him. His deportment first excited my attention. Native dignity in princes we are pleased to call barbarous was a curious spectacle. His manners were majestic, yet courteous; and he did not allow his surprise to beguile him for a moment of the composure of the monarch. He appeared to be about thirty-eight years of age, inclined to corpulence, and of a benevolent countenance. He wore a fillet of *aggry* beads around his temples, a necklace of gold cockspur shells strung by the largest ends, and over his right shoulder a red silk cord, suspending three *saphies*[7] cased in gold. His bracelets were the richest mixtures of beads and gold, and his fingers covered with rings. . . . His knee-bands were of *aggry* beads, and his ankle strings of gold ornaments of the most delicate workmanship, small drums, sankos, stools, swords, guns, and birds, clustered together. His sandals, of a soft white leather, were embossed across the instep band with small gold and silver cases of *saphies*. He was seated in a low chair, richly ornamented with gold. . . . The royal stool,[8] entirely cased in gold, was displayed under a splendid umbrella, with drums, sankos, horns, and various musical instruments, cased in gold, about the thickness of cartridge paper. Large circles of gold hung by scarlet cloth from the swords of state, the sheaths as well

[6] Brass bracelets used in trade by the Portuguese.
[7] Scraps of Muslim writing used as charms.
[8] The symbol of monarchy.

as the handles of which were also cased. Hatchets of the same were intermixed with them. The breasts of the Ocrahs,[9] and various attendants, were adorned with large stars, stools, crescents, and gossamer wings of solid gold.

14 / OBSERVATIONS ON AFRICAN SLAVERY

Most of the accounts of African slavery written by travelers deal with the mechanics of the overseas export market in slaves, and the attendant cruelties. The piece included here is from the journal of one of the greatest of English-speaking travelers to enter the interior of Africa, the Scot, Mungo Park, who reached and explored a part of the upper Niger during the years 1795, 1796, and 1797. He gives a sympathetic and objective account of slavery from the inside. When Park refers to "Africa," West Africa only should be understood, though the pattern of slavery was similar in other parts of the continent.

A state of subordination, and certain inequalities of rank and condition, are inevitable in every stage of civil society; but when this subordination is carried to so great a length that the persons and services of one part of the community are entirely at the disposal of another part, it may then be denominated a state of slavery; and in this condition of life a great body of the Negro inhabitants of Africa have continued from the most early period of their history; with this aggravation—that their children are born to no other inheritance.

The slaves in Africa, I suppose, are nearly in the proportion of three to one to the freemen. They claim no reward for their services, except food and clothing; and are treated with kindness or severity, according to the good or bad disposition of their masters. Custom, however, has established certain rules with regard to the treatment of slaves, which it is thought dishonorable to violate. Thus, the domestic slaves, or such as are born in a man's own house, are treated with more lenity than those which are purchased

From Mungo Park, *Travels in the Interior Districts of Africa* (London, 1799), pp. 287-98.

[9] Attendants, or the Okrafohene: the officials responsible for the rites of purification of the king's soul.

with money. The authority of the master over the domestic slave . . . extends only to reasonable correction; for the master cannot sell his domestic without having first brought him to a public trial before the chief men of the place. But these restrictions on the power of the master extend not to the case of prisoners taken in war, nor to that of slaves purchased with money. All these unfortunate beings are considered as strangers and foreigners, who have no right to the protection of the law, and may be treated with severity, or sold to a stranger, according to the pleasure of their owners. There are indeed regular markets where slaves of this description are brought and sold; and the value of a slave in the eye of an African purchaser increases in proportion to his distance from his native kingdom; for when slaves are only a few days' journey from the place of their nativity, they frequently effect their escape; but when one or more kingdoms intervene, escape being more difficult, they are more readily reconciled to their situation. On this account the unhappy slave is frequently transferred from one dealer to another, until he has lost all hopes of returning to his native kingdom. The slaves which are purchased by the Europeans on the coast are chiefly of this description; a few of them are collected in the petty wars, hereafter to be described, which take place near the coast; but by far the greater number are brought down in large caravans from the inland countries, of which many are unknown, even by name, to the Europeans. The slaves which are thus brought from the interior may be divided into two distinct classes: *first,* such as were slaves from their birth, having been born of enslaved mothers; *secondly,* such as were born free, but who afterwards, by whatever means, became slaves. Those of the first description are by far the most numerous; for prisoners taken in war (at least such as are taken in open and declared war, when one kingdom avows hostilities against another) are generally of this description. The comparatively small proportion of free people, to the enslaved, throughout Africa, has already been noticed; and it must be observed that men of free condition have many advantages over the slaves, even in wartime. They are in general better armed and well mounted, and can either fight or escape with some hopes of success; but the slaves, who have only their spears and bows, and of whom great numbers are loaded with baggage, become an easy prey. Thus, when Mansong, King of Bambarra, made war upon Kaarta . . . , he took in one day nine hundred prisoners, of which number not more than seventy were free men. This account I received from Daman Jumma, who had thirty slaves at Kemmoo, all of whom were made prisoners by Mansong. Again, when a freeman is taken prisoner, his friends will sometimes ransom him, by giving two slaves in exchange; but when a slave is taken, he has no hopes of such redemption. To these disadvantages it is to be added that the *slatees*,[1] who purchase slaves in the interior countries and carry them down to the coast for sale, constantly prefer such as have been in that condition of life from their infancy, well knowing that these have been accustomed to hunger and fatigue, and are better able to sustain the hardships of a long and painful journey, than free men. And on their reaching the coast, if no opportunity offers of selling them to advantage, they can easily be made to maintain themselves by their labor; neither are they so apt to attempt making their escape, as those who have once tasted the blessings of freedom.

Slaves of the second description generally become such by one or other of the following causes: 1. *captivity*; 2. *famine*; 3. *insolvency*; 4. *crimes*. A freeman may, by the established customs of Africa, become a slave by being taken in war. War is, of all others, the most productive source, and was probably the origin, of slavery; for when one nation had taken from another a greater number of captives than could be exchanged on equal terms, it is natural to suppose that the conquerors, finding it inconvenient to maintain their prisoners, would compel them to labor; at first, perhaps, only for their own support; but afterward to support their masters. Be this as it may, it is a known fact that prisoners of war in Africa are the slaves of the conquerors; and when the weak or unsuccessful warrior begs for mercy beneath the uplifted spear of his opponent, he gives up at the same time his claim to liberty, and purchases his life at the expense of his freedom. . . .

In a country divided into a thousand petty states, mostly independent and jealous of each other; where every freeman is accustomed to arms, and fond of military achievements; where the youth, who has practiced the bow and spear from his infancy, longs for

[1] Slave merchants.

nothing so much as an opportunity to display his valor, it is natural to imagine that wars frequently originate from very frivolous provocation. When one nation is more powerful than another, a pretext is seldom wanting for commencing hostilities. Thus the war between Kajaaga and Kasson was occasioned by the detention of a fugitive slave; that between Bambarra and Kaarta by the loss of a few cattle. Other cases of the same nature perpetually occur, in which the folly or mad ambition of their princes, and the zeal of their religious enthusiasts, give full employment to the scythe of desolation.

The wars of Africa are of two kinds, which are distinguished by different appellations: that species which bears the greatest resemblance to our European contests is denominated *killi*, a word signifying "to call out," because such wars are openly avowed and previously declared. Wars of this description in Africa commonly terminate, however, in the course of a single campaign. A battle is fought: the vanquished seldom think of rallying again, the whole inhabitants become panic struck, and the conquerors have only to bind the slaves, and carry off their plunder and their victims. Such of the prisoners as, through age or infirmity, are unable to endure fatigue, or are unfit for sale, are considered as useless; and I have no doubt are frequently put to death. The same fate commonly awaits a chief, or any other person who has taken a very distinguished part in the war. And here it may be observed that, notwithstanding this exterminating system, it is surprising to behold how soon an African town is rebuilt and repeopled. The circumstance arises probably from this: that their pitched battles are few; the weakest know their own situation and seek safety in flight. When their country has been desolated, and their ruined towns and villages deserted by the enemy, such of the inhabitants as have escaped the sword and the chain generally return, though with cautious steps, to the place of their nativity; for it seems to be the universal wish of mankind to spend the evening of their days where they passed their infancy. The poor Negro feels this desire in its full force. To him, no water is sweet but what is drawn from his own well; and no tree has so cool and pleasant a shade as the *tabba* tree of his native village. When war compels him to abandon the delightful spot in which he first drew his breath, and seek for safety in some other kingdom, his time is spent in talking about the country of his ancestors; and no sooner is peace restored than he turns his back upon the land of strangers, rebuilds with haste his fallen walls, and exults to see the smoke ascend from his native village.

The other species of African warfare, is distinguished by the appellation of *tegria*, "plundering or stealing." It arises from a sort of hereditary feud, which the inhabitants of one nation or district bear toward another. No immediate cause of hostility is assigned, or notice of attack given; but the inhabitants of each watch every opportunity to plunder and distress the objects of their animosity by predatory excursions. These are very common, particularly about the beginning of the dry season, when the labor of the harvest is over and provisions are plentiful. Schemes of vengeance are then meditated. The chief man surveys the number and activity of the vassals, as they brandish their spears at festivals; and elated with his own importance, turns his whole thoughts towards revenging some depredation or insult, which either he or his ancestors may have received from a neighboring state.

Wars of this description are generally conducted with great secrecy. A few resolute individuals, headed by some person of enterprise and courage, march quietly through the woods, surprise in the night some unprotected village, and carry off the inhabitants and their effects, before their neighbors can come to their assistance. One morning, during my stay at Kamalia, we were all too much alarmed by a party of this kind. The king of Fooladoo's son, with five hundred horsemen, passed secretly through the woods, a little to the southward of Kamalia, and, on the morning following, plundered three towns belonging to Madigai, a powerful chief in Jallonkadoo.

The success of this expedition encouraged the governor of Bangassi, a town in Fooladoo, to make a second inroad upon another part of the same country. Having assembled about two hundred of his people, he passed the river Kokoro in the night, and carried off a great number of prisoners. Several of the inhabitants who had escaped these attacks were afterward seized by the Mandingoes, as they wandered about in the woods, or concealed themselves in the glens and strong places of the mountains.

These plundering excursions always produce speedy retaliation and, when large parties cannot be collected for this purpose, a few friends will combine together, and advance into the enemy's country, with a view to plunder, or carry off the inhabitants. A single individual has been known to take the bow and quiver, and proceed in like manner. Such an attempt is doubtless in him an act of rashness; but when it is considered that, in one of these predatory wars, he has probably been deprived of his child or his nearest relation, his situation will rather call for pity than censure. The poor sufferer, urged on by the feelings of domestic or paternal attachment, and the ardor of revenge, conceals himself among the bushes, until some young or unarmed person passes by. He then, tiger-like, springs upon his prey, drags his victim into the thicket, and in the night carries him off as a slave.

When a Negro has, by means like these, once fallen into the hands of his enemies, he is either retained as the slave of his conqueror or bartered into a distant kingdom; for an African, when he has once subdued his enemy, will seldom give him an opportunity of lifting up his hand against him at a future period. A conqueror commonly disposes of his captives according to the rank which they held in their native kingdom. Such of the domestic slaves as appear to be of a mild disposition, and particularly the young women, are retained as his own slaves. Others that display marks of discontent, are disposed of in a distant country, and such of the freemen or slaves, as have taken an active part in the war, are either sold to the *slatees* or put to death. War, therefore, is certainly the most general, and most productive source of slavery, and the desolations of war often (but not always) produce the second cause of slavery, famine—in which case a freeman becomes a slave to avoid a greater calamity. . . .

The third cause of slavery is insolvency. Of all offences (if insolvency may be so called) to which the laws of Africa have affixed the punishment of slavery, this is the most common. A Negro trader commonly contracts debts on some mercantile speculation, either from his neighbors, to purchase such articles as will sell to advantage in a distant market, or from the European traders on the coast; payment is to be made in a given time. In both cases, the situation of the adventurer is exactly the same. If he succeeds, he may secure an independency. If he is unsuccessful, his person and services are at the disposal of another; for in Africa, not only the effects of the insolvent, but even the insolvent himself, is sold to satisfy the lawful demands of his creditors.

The fourth cause above enumerated is the commission of crimes on which the laws of the country affix slavery as a punishment. In Africa the only offences of this class are murder, adultery, and witchcraft; and I am happy to say that they did not appear to me to be common. In cases of murder, I was informed that the nearest relation of the deceased had it in his power, after conviction, either to kill the offender with his own hand, or sell him into slavery. When adultery occurs, it is generally left to the option of the person injured either to sell the culprit, or accept such a ransom as he may think equivalent to the injury he has sustained. By witchcraft is meant pretended magic by which the lives or healths of persons are affected; in other words, it is the administering of poison. No trial for this offence, however, came under my observation while I was in Africa; and I therefore suppose that the crime and its punishment occur but very seldom.

When a free man has become a slave by any one of the causes before mentioned, he generally continues so for life, and his children (if they are born of an enslaved mother) are brought up in the same state of servitude. There are however a few instances of slaves obtaining their freedom, and sometimes even with the consent of their masters; as by performing some singular piece of service, or by going to battle, and bringing home two slaves as a ransom; but the common way of regaining freedom is by escape; and when the slaves have set their minds on running away, they often succeed. Some of them will wait for years before an opportunity presents itself, and during that period show no signs of discontent. In general, it may be remarked that slaves who come from a hilly country, and have been much accustomed to hunting and travel, are more apt to attempt their escape than such as are born in a flat country, and have been employed in cultivating the land.

Such are the general outlines of that system of slavery which prevails in Africa; and it is evident, from its nature and extent, that it is a system of no modern date. It probably had its origin in the remote ages of antiquity, before the Muslims explored a path across the desert. How far it is maintained and supported by the slave traffic [which the] nations of Europe have carried on with natives of the coast, it is neither within my province, nor in my power, to explain.

PART II

15 / THE CHRISTIAN KINGDOMS OF THE UPPER NILE

Makrisi, the great Egyptian geographer and historian, who lived from 1364 to 1442, quotes extensively from a tenth-century description of Nubia and Alwa, two Christian kingdoms of the Upper Nile. The description had appeared in An Account of Nubia, Makurra, Alwa, the Begas and the Nile *by Ibn Selim al Aswani. The complete work is not in existence, and little is known of the author.*

In the description, the names Nubia and Makurra seem to alternate for the same place. The explanation is that Makurra, originally a third kingdom between Alwa and Nubia, had conquered the latter. By the tenth century, Makurra-Nubia had been one Kingdom for about four hundred years, but the Makurra-Marisi language barrier remained within it.

Abd Allah ben Ahmed ben Selim el Aswani, in his work entitled *An Account of Nubia, Makurra, Alwa, the Bejas, and the Nile,* reports as follows:

Nubia begins at the village of El Kasr, five miles from Aswan. . . . From here to the first cataract of Nubia it is ten days' journey. Muslims can settle freely in this region, and in the lower part of it they own property and trade with the upper part. A large number are established there, but none of them speak good Arabic. Trees abound, although the country is narrow and mountainous

Makrisi, *Description topographique et historique de l'Égypte.* From the French translation by U. Bouriant (Paris, 1900), pp. 549-57. Translated from the French by Caroline Oliver.

and the cultivated land ends not far from the Nile. The river is bordered with villages and one sees the palm-tree and the *moql*. The upper part of the province is larger than the lower. The vine is cultivated there. The land is too high above river to be flooded by it, and water is carried to it by means of machines worked by bullocks. In this way one, two, or three *feddans* can be irrigated. Little wheat is harvested, but barley and rye are more abundant. The cultivated strip being narrow, cultivation is forced. They restore the land in summer with manure and silt, and they sow *dokhn,* millet, sesame, and peas. Negrash, the capital of Maris, northern province of Nubia, is in this region, and the fortress of Ibrim and another fortress further north; and the port of Adowa, fatherland of the sage Lokman and of Dhul Nun, where there is a marvelous temple. The province is ruled by a Wali, who is subject to the king of Nubia, and who is called "The Lord of the Mountain." As his administrative territory touches Muslim territory in the north, he is the intermediary for Muslims who wish to trade in Nubia. He receives their merchandise and pays for it in slaves, but permits no one, whether Muslim or not, to have access to the king. . . .

Above the cataract the upper chiefdom is occupied by a garrison whose chief is directly under the king of Nubia. He guards the region so carefully that even if the king comes through, he is arrested by the garrison chief, who makes a pretence of searching him, so as to be able to search the king's son or his vizier or anyone of lesser rank. From this point on, trade is all barter. The Nubians, in fact, only use money to the north of the cataract in order to trade with Muslims. To the south of it they don't trade among themselves, but barter what they have need of against slaves, cattle, camels, iron, and grain. On pain of death, no one is allowed to pass this point without the king's permission. The result is that no one knows what is going on there, and a Nubian army can attack a neighboring country or a nomad tribe without warning. It is there that emery, which is used for polishing precious stones, is collected from the Nile. They dive into the river for it, and it is easily recognized, as it is colder than other stones. If there is any doubt, it can be recognized by blowing on it. Another cataract stretches from here to the village of Say, which is the northernmost bishopric of Nubia. There is a Nubian bishop there and also a temple. It is there that the province of Sokluda begins. The name means "Seven Walis." This region resembles the northern one in every way. It is as large and as dry, and it produces palms, vines, cereals, *moqls,* and one also sees cotton trees, from which they make a coarse material, and olive trees. The Wali is subject to the sovereign and commands his own Walis. The fortress of Astanun is in this province. It is built at the beginning of the third Nubian cataract, which is harder to pass than the others, because the course of the river here is barred by a mountain that crosses it from east to west. The Nile escapes through three openings, or two when the water is low. The waterfall makes a deafening noise and presents a magnificent spectacle. The river throws itself from the top to the bottom of the mountain. To the south of this cataract the river bed is strewn with stones for a stretch of three *barrids* to the village of Yastu, where the province of Maris ends and Makurra begins. From there to the Nubian frontier Marisi is spoken. It is the last Nubian province. It begins with the district of Bakun, which means "the marvelous," and was given to that country because of its beauty. I have not, in fact, seen another district on the banks of the Nile which is broader. As far as I could see—the river valley here—is a five-day march from east to west. . . .

After this district comes Safad Bakl, a narrow region, similar to the northern region of Nubia, except that here there are a great many fine islands. In less than two days' journey you see nearly thirty villages with pretty houses, churches, convents, palm groves, vines, gardens, fields, and stretching meadows, where cattle and excellent reddish colored camels graze. The king often comes here, because Dongola, the capital of the country, is in the south of this district. From Dongola to Aswan is fifty days' journey. The author describes Dongola, and adds; "For the roofs of the dwellings they use wooden beams that the Nile carries down in flood, already trimmed. No one knows where they come from. I myself saw some strange marks on one of them. From Dongola to the frontier of Alwa is farther than from Dongola to Aswan."

The Nubians and the Makurra are two distinct people. They do not speak the same language, but both of them live on the banks of the Nile. The Nubians are no other than the Marisi, who live in the neighborhood of the Muslim countries. . . .

They say that Selha, ancestor of the Nubians, and Makurri, ancestor of the Makurras, came originally from the Yemen. There are others who think that both Nubians and Makurra are Himyarites, but most genealogists are of the opinion that they descend from Ham, son of Noah. They fought each other before the appearance of Christianity. . . .

The country of Alwa begins at a village called El Abuab (the gates), on the east bank of the river. It is under a Wali who is subject to the king of Alwa, and who has the title of Rahrah. Above here the Nile divides into seven branches. One of them, which comes from the east, carries a muddy water. It is dry during the summer, and the bed is then inhabited. . . .

The second river is the White Nile, which comes from the west, and the waters of which are as white as milk. I interrogated a traveler who had been through the land of the blacks, about the course and the color of the river that waters this country. This is what he told me: "The river comes out of sandy mountains and flows through immense lakes, situated in the land of the blacks. . . . The third river is the Green i.e., [blue], Nile which comes from the southeast.

Soba, the capital of Alwa, is on the east of the great island formed by the White and Green rivers, and at the northern end of it, at the confluence of the two rivers. To the east of the town is the river that is inhabited when its bed dries up. There are some lovely buildings to be seen in the town, vast convents, churches with a great deal of gold in them, and gardens. Muslims live in one of the suburbs. The king of Alwa is richer than the king of Makurra [Nubia], has more horses and more soldiers, and his country is larger and more fertile. Palms and vines are rare. The heaviest crop is *durra,* which is like rice. They make bread and beer out of it. There is plenty of meat there, because cattle abound, as the meadows there are so vast that the mountains are several days' march away. The country produces good horses, and red-skinned Arab camels. The people are Jacobite Christians.[1] As with the Nubians, their bishops are sent to them by the patriarch of Alexandria. They use Greek books that they translate into their own language. They are less intelligent than the Nubians. Their king is absolute master and reduces his subjects to slavery as he

[1] Christians belonging to the Coptic Church.

pleases, whether they are innocent or guilty. Far from protesting, the man so treated prostrates himself before the master, and without complaining of the injustice he suffers, cries:—"Long live the King! His will be done!" The king wears a gold crown, for gold is very abundant in the country.

16 / RECEPTION OF A PORTUGUESE EMBASSY AT THE ETHIOPIAN COURT IN 1520

By the fifteenth century, when the Portuguese were exploring the coast of Africa, the legendary Christian kingdom of the Prester John had come to be identified with Ethiopia. The Portuguese, hoping to find an ally against the Muslim world, sent various envoys to the Ethiopian court, which, in return, sent an envoy to Portugal. Subsequently, in 1520 during the reign of the Emperor Lebna Dengel, a large Portuguese mission arrived in Ethiopia, where it stayed for six years. The party consisted of Dom Rodrigo de Lima, the ambassador, and thirteen companions. One of them, Father Francisco Alvares, wrote an account of the mission in A True Relation of the Lands of the Prester John, *a work of some historical importance, as it is the only eyewitness account of Ethiopia in the days of its medieval splendor. In the second half of the sixteenth century, Ethiopia suffered considerable disruption as a result of invasions from the east and south by Somali and Galla.*

On Tuesday we were all summoned—that is to say, the ambassador and those who were with him; we went and stayed before the first gate or entrance a good three hours; it was very cold indeed and quite night. We passed through the enclosures as we had done twice before. There were many more people assembled than on any of the other times, and many with arms, and many more lighted candles before the gates; and they did not detain us there long, but soon bade us enter with the ambassador, nine Portuguese, beyond the curtains. Beyond these first curtains we found others still richer, and they bade us pass through these also. Having passed these last we found a large and rich dais with very splendid car-

Francisco Alvares, *A True Relation of the Lands of the Prester John.* From *The Prester John of the Indies,* ed. C. F. Beckingham and G. W. B. Huntingford (Hakluyt Society Publication, Series II, number cxiv, 1961), Vol. I, pp. 303-305. Reprinted by permission of Cambridge University Press.

pets. In front of this dais were other curtains of much greater splendor, and while we were standing before them they opened them, for they were drawn together, and there we saw the Prester John sitting on a platform of six steps very richly adorned. He had on his head a high crown of gold and silver—that is to say, one piece of gold and another of silver from the top downward, and a silver cross in his hand; there was a piece of blue taffeta before his face which covered his mouth and beard, and from time to time they lowered it and the whole of his face appeared, and again they raised it. At his right hand he had a page dressed in silk, with a flat silver cross in his hand, with figures carved in it with a burin; from where we stood it was not possible to make out these figures on the cross, but I saw it later, and saw the figures. The Prester was dressed in a rich mantle of gold brocade, and silk shirts of wide sleeves which looked like *pelotes*.[1] From his knees downward he had a rich cloth of silk and gold well spread out like a bishop's apron, and he was sitting in majesty as they paint God the Father on the wall. Besides the page with the cross, there stood on each side of him another, dressed in the same way, each with a drawn sword in his hand. In age, complexion, and stature, he is a young man, not very black. His complexion might be chestnut or bay, not very dark in color; he is very much a man of breeding, of middling stature; they said that he was twenty-three years of age, and he looks like that. His face is round, the eyes large, the nose high in the middle, and his beard is beginning to grow. In presence and state he fully looks like the great lord that he is. We were about two lances distant from him. Messages came and went all through the *cabeata*.[2] On each side of the platform were four pages richly dressed, each with lighted candles in their hands. When the questions and answers were ended, the ambassador gave to the *cabeata* the letters and instructions of the captain major, put into their letters and language; and he gave them to the Prester, who read them very speedily. . . .

[1] Jerkins.
[2] The highest court official who arranged the councils.

17 / THE CITY OF AKSUM IN THE SIXTEENTH CENTURY

Aksum, the ancient capital of Ethiopia, was founded by Semitic immigrants from southwest Arabia at the beginning of the Christian era. Alvarez[1] prefaces his description of it with the legendary story of the visit of the queen of Sheba to King Solomon in Jerusalem, and of their union which is said to have given Ethiopia a great dynasty. He also gives the story of the bringing of Christianity to Ethiopia by St. Philip the Apostle, although, in fact, the conversion of the kingdom to Christianity probably took place in the fourth century A.D.

Amongst these peaks, between which we were still going, to the west are wonderful lands and very great lordships, among which is a very great town named Aksum, and it is two days' journey from the town of St. Michael, always between these peaks. We stayed in it for eight months by order of the Prester John. This town was the city, court, and residence of the Queen Sheba, who took the camels laden with gold to Solomon, when he was building the temple of Jerusalem. There is in this town a very noble church, in which we found a very long chronicle written in the language of the country, and it stated at the very beginning that it had been written first in Hebrew, and afterward put into Greek, and from Greek into Chaldean, and from Chaldean into Abyssinian,[2] which it now is, and it begins thus:

How the Queen Sheba hearing related the great and rich buildings which Solomon had begun in Jerusalem, determined to go and see them; and she loaded camels with gold to give for these buildings. And on arriving near the city, and being about to cross a lake, which they passed by a bridge of boats, she dismounted and worshipped the beams and said: "Please God my feet shall not touch the timber on which the Saviour of the world has to hang." And she went round the lake, and went to see Solomon, and begged him to take away those beams from there, and she came to the

Francisco Alvares, *A True Relation of the Lands of the Prester John*. From *The Prester John of the Indies*, ed. C. F. Beckingham and G. W. B. Huntingford (Hakluyt Society Publication, Series II, number cxiv, 1961), Vol. I, pp. 145-61. Reprinted by permission of Cambridge University Press.

[1] See introduction to extract 16.
[2] Amharic.

buildings, and offered her gifts and said: "These buildings are not such as they told me in richness and beauty, because their beauty and richness has no equal, so that they are greater than what was related to me, so much so that the tongues of men cannot tell their nobility and richness, and much I grieve for the small gift which I brought. I will return to my countries and lordships, and I will send whatever abounds for the buildings, of gold, and black wood [3] to inlay." While she was at Jerusalem Solomon had intercourse with her, and she became pregnant of a son, and remained at Jerusalem until she gave him birth. After she was able to travel she left her son,[4] and returned to her country, and sent from it much gold and black wood to inlay the buildings. And her son grew up to the age of seventeen years, and among the many sons that Solomon had, this one was so proud that he affronted the people of Israel, and all the country of Judea. And the people came to Solomon and said to him: "We are not able to maintain so many kings as you have got, for all your sons are kings, especially this one of Queen Sheba; she is a greater lady than you; send him to his mother, for we are not able to maintain him." Then Solomon sent him very honorably, giving him the officers that are usual in a king's household, and besides, he gave him, in order that he might rest on the road, the country of Gaza, which is in Egypt; and he made his journey to the country of his mother, where he was a great ruler. The chronicle says that he ruled from sea to sea, and that he had sixty ships in the Indian sea. This book of chronicles is very large, and I copied only the beginning.

In this town of Aksum was the principal residence of Queen Candace who was the beginning of the country's being Christian. She was born (as they say) half a league from here, in a very small village, which now is entirely of blacksmiths. The beginning of her being Christian was this. According to what they say in their books, the angel said to Philip[5]: "Rise and go toward the south, by the road which goes from Jerusalem to Gaza, the desert." St. Philip went and met with a man who was a eunuch, and he was major-domo of the Queen Candace, ruler of Ethiopia. In the country of

---

[3] Ebony.

[4] Menelik, called Ebna Hakim, "Son of the Wise."

[5] St. Philip the Apostle.

Gaza, which Solomon had given to his son, this man was the keeper of all the riches of the queen, and he had been to Jerusalem and was returning to his house, and he was going on a chariot. St. Philip came up to him, and heard him sing a prophecy of Isaiah, and asked him how he understood what he was singing. He replied that he did not know, unless some other man taught him. St. Philip mounted into the chariot, and went on explaining to him that prophecy, and converted him, and baptized and instructed him in the faith. Then the Spirit snatched away St. Philip, and he was perfectly instructed. They say that here was fulfilled the prophecy which David spoke: "Ethiopia shall arise, and stretch forth her hands to God." So they say they were the first Christians in the world. The eunuch at once set out very joyfully for Ethiopia, where was the house of his mistress, and converted her and all her household, and baptized them in consequence of what he related to them. And the queen caused all her kingdom, beginning with a kingdom which is now called the kingdom of Buno, to be baptized. This Buno is toward the east from the town of Aksum in the kingdom of the Barnagais, and it is now two lordships. In this town of Aksum, where she became Christian, she built a very noble church, the first there was in Ethiopia: it is named St. Mary of Zion.[6] They say that it is so named because its altar stone came from Zion. In this country they have the custom always to name the churches by the altar stone, because on it is written the name of the patron saint. This stone which they have in this church, they say that the Apostles sent it from Mount Zion. This church is very large. It has five aisles of good width and of great length, vaulted above, and all the vaults closed; the ceiling and sides are painted. Below, the body of the church is well worked with handsome cut stones; it has seven chapels, all with their backs to the east, and their altars well ornamented. It has a choir after our fashion, except that it is low, and they reach the vaulted roof with their heads; and the choir is also over the vault, and they do not use it. This church has a very large circuit, paved with flagstones like the lids of tombs. This consists of a very high wall, and it is not covered over like those of the other churches, but it is left open. This church has a large enclosure, and it is also surrounded

[6] The Cathedral church of Aksum, the holiest church in Ethiopia.

by another larger enclosure, like the enclosing wall of a large town or city. Within this enclosure are handsome groups of one-story buildings, and all spout out their water by strong figures of lions and dogs of stone. Inside this large enclosure there are two mansions, one on the right hand and the other on the left, which belong to two rectors of the church: and the other houses are of canons and monks. In the large enclosure, at the gate nearest the church, there is a large ruin, built in a square, which in other times was a house, and it has at each corner a big stone pillar, squared and worked. This house is called Ambacabete, which means house of lions. They say that in this house were the captive lions, and there are still some always traveling, and there go before the Prester John four captive lions. Before the gate of this great enclosure there is a large court, and in it a large tree, which they call Pharaoh's fig tree, and at each end of it there are some very new looking pedestals of masonry well worked, laid down. Only where they reach near the foot of the fig tree, they are injured by the roots, which raise them up. There are, on the top of these pedestals, twelve stone chairs as well made with stone as though they were of wood, with their seats and rests for the feet. They are not made out of a block, but each one from its own stone and separate piece. They say these belong to the twelve judges who at this time serve in the court of the Prester John. Outside this enclosure there is a large town of very good houses, such that there are none like them in the whole of Ethiopia, and very good wells of water, of worked masonry, and also in most of the houses the before-mentioned ancient figures of lions, dogs, and birds, all well made in stone. At the back of this great church is a very handsome tank of masonry, and upon this masonry are as many other chairs of stone, such as those in the enclosure of the church. This town is situated at the head of a beautiful plain, and almost between two hills, and the rest of this plain is almost all full of these old buildings, and among them many of these chairs, and high pillars with inscriptions. Above this town there are many stones[7] standing up, and others on the ground, very large and beautiful, and worked with beautiful designs, among which is one raised upon another, and worked like an altar stone, except that it is of very great size, and it is set in the other as if enchased.

[7] The obelisks.

Above this town, on a hill which overlooks much distant country, and which is about a mile, that is the third of a league, from the town, there are two houses under the ground, into which men do not enter without a lamp. These houses are not vaulted, but of very good straight masonry, both the walls and the roof. The blocks are free on the outside; the walls may be twelve *covados*[8] high; the blocks are set in the wall so close one to the other, that it all looks like one stone. One of these houses is much divided into chambers and granaries; in the doorways are holes for the bars and for the sockets of the doors. In one of these chambers are two very large chests, each one four *covados* in length, and one and a half broad, and as much in overall height, and in the upper part on the inner side they are hollowed at the edge, as though they had lids of stone, as the chests also are of stone. (They say they were the treasure chests of Queen Sheba. . . .) There were in our company Genoese and Catalans, who had been prisoners of the Turks, and they affirmed and swore that they had seen Troy, and the granary of Joseph in the kingdom of Egypt, and that their buildings were very large, but that these of this town were and are altogether much larger, and it seemed to us that the Prester John had sent us here, in order that we should see these buildings, and we had rejoiced at seeing them, as they are much greater than what I write. . . .

As they say the church of Aksum is the most ancient, so it is the most revered of all Ethiopia: and the services are well conducted in it. In this church there are one hundred and fifty canons, and as many monks. It has two head men, one is named *nebrete* of the canons, which means teacher, and the other *nebrete* of the monks. These two heads reside in the palaces which are within the great enclosure and circuit of the church: and the *nebrete* of the canons lodges at the right hand, and he is the principal one, and the more respected. He has jurisdiction over the canons and the laity of all this country: and the *nebrete* of the monks only hears and rules the monks. Both use kettledrums and trumpets. They have very large revenues, and besides their revenues they have every day a collation which they call *maabar* of bread and wine of the country, when mass is finished. The monks have this by themselves, and the canons also, and this *maabar* is such that

[8] One covado = 27 inches.

the monks seldom eat other food than that. They have this every day except Friday of the Passion, because on that day no one eats or drinks. The canons do not take their *maabar* within the circuit of the church, and are seldom there, except at fixed hours, neither is the *nebrete* in his palace, except at some chance time when he goes to hear cases. This is because they are married, and live with their wives and children in their houses, which are very good and which are outside. Neither women nor laymen go into the enclosure of this church, and they do not go in to receive the communion.[9] On account of their being married, and because the women do not enter the circuit, they take their *maabar* outside, so that their wives and children may enjoy it.

18 / RITES AND CUSTOMS OF THE ETHIOPIAN CROWN

The great Scottish gentleman, James Bruce of Kinnaird, traveled extensively in northeast Africa between 1768 and 1773, visiting Ethiopia just over two hundred and fifty years after Alvares.[1] While searching for the sources of the Nile, he compiled material for his five erudite volumes descriptive of the whole region which were published in 1790.

The crown of Abyssinia[2] is hereditary, and has always been so, in one particular family, supposed to be that of Solomon by the queen of Sheba, Negesta Azab, or queen of the south. It is nevertheless elective in this line; and there is no law of the land, nor custom, which gives the eldest son an exclusive title to succeed to his father. The practice has indeed been quite the contrary. When, at the death of a king, his sons are old enough to govern, and, by some accident, not yet sent prisoners to the mountain,[3] then the eldest, or he that is next, or he that is not confined, generally takes possession of the throne by the strength of his father's friends. But

From James Bruce, *Travels to Discover the Source of the Nile* (Edinburgh, 1790), Vol. III, pp. 262-74.

[9] There was another church where the laity and the women received the communion.

[1] See extract 16.

[2] Bruce uses the Arabic name Abyssinia which means "land of slaves," and is much disliked by the Ethiopians.

[3] The possible heirs to the throne were confined at some distance from the capital on a mountain top.

if no heir is then in the low country, the choice of the king is always according to the will of the minister, which passes for that of the people. And, his inclination and interest being to govern, he never fails to choose an infant whom thereafter he directs, ruling the kingdom absolutely during the minority, which generally exhausts, or is equal to the term of his life.

From this flow all the misfortunes of this unhappy country. This very defect arises from a desire to institute a more than ordinarily perfect government; for the Abyssinians' first position was, "Woe be to the kingdom whose king is a child": and this they know must often happen when succession is left to the course of nature. But when there was a choice to be made out of two hundred persons all of the same family, all capable of reigning, it was their own fault, they thought, if they had not always a prince of proper age and qualification to rule the kingdom, according to the necessities of the times, and to preserve the succession of the family in the house of Solomon, agreeable to the laws of the land. And indeed, it has been this manner of reasoning, good at first view, though found afterward but too fallacious, which has ruined their kingdom in part, and often brought the whole into the utmost hazard and jeopardy.

The king is anointed with plain oil of olives, which, being poured upon the crown of his head, he rubs into his long hair indecently enough with both hands, pretty much as his soldiers do with theirs when they get access to plenty of butter. The crown is made in the shape of a priest's mitre, or headpiece; it is a kind of helmet, covering the king's forehead, cheeks, and neck. It is lined with blue taffeta; the outside is half gold and half silver, of the most beautiful filigrane work.

The crown in Joa's time was burnt, with part of the palace. . . . The present [one] was since made by the Greeks from Smyrna, who have large appointments here, and work with very great taste and elegance, though they have not near so much encouragement as formerly.

On the top of the crown was a ball of red glass, or crystal, with several bells of different colors within it. It seems to me to have formerly been no better than part of the stopper of a glass decanter. Be that as it may, it was lost in Yasous's time at the defeat of Sennaar. It was found, however, by a Muslim and brought by

Guangoul, chief of the Bertuma Galla, to the frontiers of Tigre, where Michael, governor of that province, went with an army in great ceremony to receive it, and, returning with it, gave it to King Yasous, making thereby a great advance toward the king's favor.

Some people, among the other unwarranted things they have advanced, have said that at the king's coronation a gold earring is put into his ears, and a drawn sword into his hand, and all the people fall down and worship him. But there is no such ceremony in use, and exhibitions of this kind, made by the king in public, at no period seem to have suited the genius of this people. Formerly his face was never seen, nor any part of him, excepting sometimes his foot. He sits in a kind of balcony, with lattice windows and curtains before him. Even yet he covers his face on audiences or public occasions, and when in judgment. On cases of treason he sits within his balcony, and speaks through a hole in the side of it to an officer called *kal-hatze*,[4] the "voice or word of the king," by whom he sends his questions, or anything else that occurs, to the judges that are seated at the council table.

The king goes to church regularly, his guards taking possession of every avenue and door through which he is to pass, and nobody is allowed to enter with him, because he is then on foot, excepting two officers of his bedchamber who support him. He kisses the threshold and side-posts of the church door, the steps before the altar, and then returns home. Sometimes there is a service in the church, sometimes there is not; but he takes no notice of the difference. He rides upstairs into the presence chamber on a mule, and lights immediately on the carpet before his throne; and I have sometimes seen great indecencies committed by the said mule in the presence chamber, upon a Persian carpet.

An officer called *serach massery*, with a long whip, begins cracking and making a noise, worse than twenty French postillions, at the door of the palace before the dawn of day. This chases away the hyena and other wild beasts. This, too, is the signal for the king's rising, who sits in judgment every morning fasting, and after that, about eight o'clock, he goes to breakfast.

There are six noblemen of the king's own choosing, who are *baalomaal*, or gentlemen of the bedchamber; four of these are

[4] Compare the *cabeata* mentioned by Alvares, extract 16.

always with him. There is a seventh who is the chief of these, called *azelessa el camisha,* groom of the robe or stole. He is keeper of the king's wardrobe, and the first officer of the bedchamber. These officers, the black slaves, and some others serve him as menial servants, and are in a degree of familiarity with him, unknown to the rest of his subjects.

When the king sits to consult upon civil matters of consequence, he is shut up in a kind of box opposite to the head of the council table. The persons that deliberate sit at the table, and, according to their rank, give their voices, the youngest or lowest officer always speaking first. The first that give their votes are the *shalaka,* or colonels of the household troops. The second are the great butlers, men that have the charge of the king's drink. The third is the *badjerund,* or keeper of that apartment in the palace called the lion's house. . . .

[*A long list of court officials has been omitted.*]

After the governor of Tigre comes the *acab saat,* or guardian of the fire, and the chief ecclesiastical officer of the king's household. Some have said that this office was appointed to attend the king at the time of eating, and that it was his province to order both meat and drink to be withdrawn whenever he saw the king inclined to excess. If this was really his office, he never used it in my time, nor, as far as I could learn, for several reigns before. Besides, no king eats in public, or before any person but slaves; and he never would choose that time to commit excess, in which he might be controlled by a subject, even if it was that subject's right to be present when the king eats, as it is not.

After the *acab saat* comes the first master of the household; then the *betwudet,* or *ras;* last of all the king gives his sentence, which is final, and sends it to the table from the balcony where he is then sitting, by the officer called, as aforementioned, *kal-hatze.*

It is the constant practice in Abyssinia to beset the king's doors and windows within his hearing, and there, from early morning to night, to cry for justice as loud as possible, in a distressed and complaining tone, and in all the different languages they are masters of, in order to their being admitted to have their supposed grievances heard. In a country so ill-governed as Abyssinia is, and so perpetually involved in war, it may be easily supposed there is no want of people who have real injuries and violence to complain of. But if it were not so, this is so much the constant usage, that when it happens (as in the midst of the rainy season) that few people can approach the capital, or stand without in such bad weather, a set of vagrants are provided, maintained, and paid, whose sole business it is to cry and lament, as if they had been really very much injured and oppressed. And this they tell you is for the king's honor, that he may not be lonely by the palace being too quiet. This, of all their absurd customs, was the most grievous and troublesome to me; and, from a knowledge that it was so, the king, when he was private, often permitted himself a piece of rather odd diversion to be a royal one.

There would sometimes, while I was busy in my room in the rainy season, be four or five hundred people, who all at once would begin, some roaring and crying as if they were in pain, others demanding justice as if they were that moment suffering, or if in the instant to be put to death; and some groaning and sobbing as if just expiring; and this horrid symphony was so artfully performed that no ear could distinguish but that it proceeded from real distress. I was often so surprised as to send the soldiers at the door to bring in one of them, thinking him come from the country, to examine who had injured him. And many a time he was a servant of my own, or some other equally known; or, if he was a stranger, upon asking what misfortune had befallen him, he would answer very composedly [that] nothing was the matter with him; that he had been sleeping all day with the horses; that hearing from the soldiers at the door I was retired to my apartment, he and his companions had come to cry and make a noise under my window to do me *honor* before the people, for fear I should be melancholy by being too quiet when alone; and therefore hoped that I would order them drink, that they might continue with a little more spirit. The violent anger which this did often put me into did not fail to be punctually reported to the king, at which he would laugh heartily; and he himself was often hid not far off, for the sake of being a spectator of my heavy displeasure.

19 / AN ETHIOPIAN LOVE FEAST

In the capital, where one is safe from surprise at all times, or in the country or villages, when the rains have become so constant that the valleys will not bear a horse to pass them, or that men cannot venture far from home through fear of being surrounded and swept away by the temporary torrents occasioned by sudden showers on the mountains; in a word, when a man can say he is safe at home, and the spear and shield is hung up in the hall, a number of people of the best fashion in the villages, of both sexes, courtiers in the palace, or citizens in the town, meet together to dine between twelve and one o'clock.

A long table is set in the middle of a large room, and benches beside it for a number of guests who are invited. Tables and benches the Portuguese introduced amongst them; but bull hides spread upon the ground served them before, as they do in the camp and country now. A cow or bull, one or more, as the company is numerous, is brought close to the door. . . .

[*There follows a detailed description of the carving up of the beast, which was commenced while it was still alive.*]

The prodigious noise the animal makes is the signal for the company to sit down to table.

There are then laid before every guest—instead of plates—pancake, and something thicker and tougher. It is unleavened bread of a sourish taste, far from being disagreeable, and very easily digested, made of a grain called *teff*. It is of different colors, from black to the color of the whitest wheat-bread. Three or four of these cakes are generally put uppermost, for the food of the person opposite to whose seat they are placed. Beneath these are four or five of ordinary bread, and of a blackish kind. These serve the master to wipe his fingers upon; and afterwards the servant, for bread to his dinner.

Two or three servants then come, each with a square piece of beef in their bare hands, laying it upon the cakes of *teff*, placed like dishes down the table, without cloth or anything else beneath

From James Bruce, *Travels to Discover the Source of the Nile* (Edinburgh 1790), Vol. III, pp. 301-305.

them. By this time all the guests have knives in their hands, and their men have the large crooked ones, which they put to all sorts of uses during the time of war. The women have small clasped knives, such as the worst of the kind made at Birmingham, sold for a penny each.

The company are so ranged that one man sits between two women; the man with his long knife cuts a thin piece, which would be thought a good beefsteak in England, while you see the motion of the fibers yet perfectly distinct, and alive in the flesh. No man in Abyssinia, of any fashion whatever, feeds himself or touches his own meat. The women take the steak and cut it lengthways like strings, about the thickness of your little finger, then crossways into square pieces, something smaller than dice. This they lay upon a piece of *teff* bread, strongly powdered with black pepper, and fossile-salt; they then wrap it up in the *teff* bread like a cartridge.

In the meantime the man, having put up his knife, with each hand resting upon his neighbor's knee, his body stooping, his head low and forward, and mouth open very like an idiot, turns to the one whose cartridge is first ready, who stuffs the whole of it into his mouth, which is so full that he is in constant danger of being choked. This is a mark of grandeur. The greater the man would seem to be, the larger piece he takes in his mouth; and the more noise he makes in chewing it, the more polite he is thought to be. They have, indeed, a proverb that says, "Beggars and thieves only eat small pieces, or without making a noise." Having dispatched this morsel, which he does very expeditiously, his next female neighbor holds forth another cartridge, which goes the same way, and so on till he is satisfied. He never drinks till he has finished eating; and, before he begins, in gratitude to the fair ones that feed him, he makes up two small rolls of the same kind and form; each of his neighbors open their mouths at the same time, while with each hand he puts their portions into their mouths. He then falls to drinking out of a handsome horn; the ladies eat till they are satisfied, and then all drink together. "Vive la joie et la jeunesse!" A great deal of mirth and joke goes round, very seldom with any mixture of acrimony or ill-humor. . . .

[*The beast is then torn to pieces and finished off by the people outside the door.*]

In the meantime, those within are very much elevated; love lights all its fires, and everything is permitted with absolute freedom. There is no coyness, no delays, no need of appointments or retirement to gratify their wishes; there are no rooms but one, in which they sacrifice both to Bacchus and to Venus. The two men nearest the vacuum a pair have made on the bench by leaving their seats, hold their upper garments like a screen before the two that have left the bench; and, if we may judge by sound, they seem to think it is as great a shame to make love in silence as to eat.—Replaced in their seats again, the company drink the happy couple's health; and their example is followed at different ends of the table, as each couple is disposed. All this passes without remark or scandal, not a licentious word is uttered, nor the most distant joke upon the transaction.

20 / KABAKA JUKO I AND PRINCE KAYEMBA OF BUGANDA

Since the introduction of literacy to Africa the traditional history of African states, which formerly had been passed on orally from generation to generation, has been to some extent recorded and published. This history, consisting generally of colorful legends built around a historical thread of variable authenticity, very often exists in such abundance that story can be tried against story, and then further tried against the oral tradition of neighboring states, so that a considerable degree of historical truth emerges. The material is similar to that used in England by the Venerable Bede in the eighth century.

The chapter of Buganda history given here is from the vernacular work on the Kabakas of Buganda by Apolo Kagwa, a Buganda chief. It is translated into English by Mr. M. S. M. Kiwanuka, himself a Muganda, in his as yet unpublished work on the oral tradition of Buganda.

Buganda is the largest state in modern Uganda.

Juko succeeded his half-brother Mutebbe as king. When the funeral rites were completed, and the mourning ceremonies over, the new king built himself a capital on Ngalamye Hill. A year

Apolo Kago Kagwa, *Ekitabo kya Busekabaka be Buganda* (London: Sheldon Press for the Uganda Bookshop, Kampala, 1927). From the translation (unpublished) by M. S. M. Kiwanuka.

after his accession to the throne, the king contracted a disease that sent him mad. His subjects took him to Bumbu where there was a medicine man. The king was soon cured of his malady, and he was made to undergo a purification ceremony. This was as follows: the medicine man washed the whole of the king's body with herbs. Then they brought a banana tree and cut it lengthwise without completely splitting it. After this, they covered the king's head with a piece of bark-cloth and made him walk through the banana tree. As he went through, the bark-cloth got stuck in the banana tree.

When the king was completely cured, he left Bumbu and went to Mawula Hill, where he made a new capital. After he had been there a few days, he was told that there was a wonderfully beautiful girl at Nabutitti. She belonged to the Nvuma clan, and her name was Nalugga. The king went and proposed to her, and she accepted him. Then he married her. Soon after his marriage the king built another capital at Lubaga, where he lived for many years. When he fell ill, he left Lubaga and built another capital on Wagaba Hill, where he also lived for a long time.

One day when he was going round his capital, the king saw a medicine man giving a charm to a young prince, and reprimanded him. However, the medicine man replied boldly that the charm was good for the young prince's health. The king was angered, and he wished to put the medicine man in the stocks. At this the medicine man threatened that if he was arrested he would make the sun to fall down and refuse to give light. Before the king answered the sun set suddenly and darkness enveloped the whole world.[1] When the chief wife, Nalugga, saw that the sun had set and that there was darkness all over the earth, she advised the king to go and call the priest of the god, Wanga, and ask him "to hang up the sun for us." When the priest came he pronounced several oracles to the king, and then finally restored the sun to its proper place again. King Juko, who must have been very grateful, entrusted the care of his two children to the medicine man. They were Prince Kyekaba and Princess Kagere.

It is alleged that the sun fell on Bakka Hill, but I do not think

[1] Buganda was in the line of a total eclipse of the sun in 1680. According to the generations, this date would fall in Kabaka Juko's reign.

this story is true. Probably the ancients did not know exactly what happened.

While King Juko was in his capital, some priests came and told him to warn his brother, Prince Kayemba, not to marry the girl he was then courting. The priest prophesied that if he married her the whole royal family would die. The king, therefore, sent a warning to his brother not to marry Nakku, "because the gods advised against the marriage." Kayemba, however, sent a reply with the royal messengers: "Why was it that the gods did not prevent you from marrying Nalugga?" After this defiant answer, Prince Kayemba went ahead and married Nakku. When King Juko saw that his brother had defied the advice of the gods, he plotted to kill him. He conspired with a man called Masakate, who was responsible for the building of the royal canoes. Masakate was sent to Bulama to tell the chiefs to make a canoe of clay, and to decorate it elaborately with cowrie shells. When the canoe was made and decorated, Masakate returned to the capital, and reported that all was ready.

King Juko's next move was to plan a hostile expedition to the islands of Buvuma,[2] and to appoint his brother, Kayemba, as leader of the expedition. At this time princes were still trusted to lead war expeditions without fear of their rebelling. Prince Kayemba accepted the appointment, swore the oath of allegiance to his brother, and set off. When he reached Kisubi he heard a herd-boy playing a flute. Kayemba stopped and listened to the song which went like this: "One who does not listen to warnings will embark in a canoe made of clay. Kayemba has a leprosy behind his neck, but he is not aware of it."

When Kayemba heard this he asked what it was all about. Then someone warned him that there was a conspiracy to make him embark in a canoe made of clay. He also pretended that he was not aware of the leprosy that was eating away his neck. He touched it, and asked his retainers to tell him if it was really there. They told him it was, and that they had not told him about it before, as they were afraid of him.

When the chiefs of Bulama brought the canoes for the expedition, Kayemba refused to embark in the decorated one. Instead

[2] See introduction to extract 21.

he made Masakate, the man who was responsible for making it, sail in that particular canoe. Before Masakate was a few leagues away the canoe melted and he sank with it. Kayemba himself embarked in one of the other canoes made of wood. The men who made the clay canoe had a very difficult task, because it had to resemble exactly one of the wooden canoes.

The war-fleet sailed and called at many places on the way. The army slept at Nkumba, Nsanji, Lwajje, Naluma's, Bulutwe, and finally Bugolo. They reached Buvuma the day after leaving Bugolo. Before they arrived at Buvuma, the commander told the ones who would be arriving first to stand on one leg when they landed. When the islanders saw just a few invaders arriving in small bands, and that they all seemed to be lame, they had a council of war and decided to wait till all the enemy forces had landed, and then swoop and annihilate them. The islanders' tactics proved wrong, for when all the Buganda forces had landed and fighting began, the islanders suffered a crushing defeat and many were killed. These procrastinating tactics of the Bavuma gave rise to the ancient saying:— "Linda baware Yawanguza Buvuma." (The idea of waiting to fight the enemy when all his forces have gathered resulted in the defeat of the Bavuma.) If they had engaged the small bands of Baganda that arrived first, they would never have been defeated on their own ground.

After the battle, Kayemba decided to settle on the island, because he was afraid of returning to Buganda, where his brother, the king, was plotting to kill him. In the meantime his wife conceived. Then a medium came, who warned Kayemba that if his wife gave birth while they were still on the island, they would both die. Their death would be the result of his marrying Nakku against the advice of the gods. When Kayemba heard these warnings once again, he decided to divorce Nakku. She was therefore taken to Chief Luba in Busoga.[3] The people of Busoga were astonished to see a Muganda woman without an escort, especially as she was pregnant. The Basoga consulted a medicine man, who advised them to return the woman to her husband. But when they returned her to Kayemba in Buvuma, he told them that he did not love her, and also denied that he was her husband. He told the Basoga to take her to Buganda, and even threatened to fight them

[3] See introduction to extract 21.

f they refused. When Chief Luba saw that Kayemba was deter-
nined not to have his wife back, he chose some men to escort her
ack to Buganda. But before they reached Jinja, Nakku gave
irth to a limbless baby. She was so shocked that she called the
aby Kawumpuli.[4]

Nakku had a midwife who was a medium of the goddess Nabu-
ana. This woman, who was a Munyoro,[5] was ordered to carry the
aby. When the party reached Jinja they failed to get canoes to
arry them across to Buganda. They went to Bugaya, another island
n the lake, and got a canoe called Nakakweya. From Jinja they
vent to a village called Busawuli in Bulondoganyi, where the baby,
ts mother, and the midwife remained. The birth of Kawumpuli
vas the beginning of the custom whereby Munyoro women, who
re mediums to the goddess Nabuzana, became the traditional
ursemaids of Baganda princess and princesses.

When King Juko learned that Kayemba had divorced his wife,
nd that the latter and the limbless baby were in Bulondoganyi,
e consulted with his chiefs to decide what should be done. The
ing's main cause for anxiety was that Prince Kayemba not only
efused to return to Buganda, but that he kept the army with
vhich he had conquered Buvuma there with him. The king there-
ore devised a plan whereby he could lure his brother back to
Buganda. He ordered all the inhabitants of Kyaggwe[6] to stop cul-
ivating their gardens and let the land go wild, and also to stop
utting their hair, as though they were in mourning. He then
moved his capital to a place called Bujuko, and commissioned
Mulwana, his prime minister, to go to Buvuma to tell Kayemba
that his brother was dead, and that he should return to Buganda
nd succeed to the throne.

When Mulwana reached Buvuma and told his story, Kayemba at
once smelled a rat and was not taken in. But he sent some of his
own retainers to the mainland to ascertain if the king were dead.
When they reached Kyaggwe they found the whole countryside
uncultivated and the people wearing their hair long as though in
mourning. They returned and reported to their master that the

---

[4] Kawumpuli means the "god of the plague," or, metaphorically, a "much
dreaded person."

[5] A woman of Bunyoro in western Uganda.

[6] A Buganda county on the north shore of Lake Victoria.

country was in a state of mourning, and therefore Mulwana's story that the king was dead must be true. On getting this evidence from his own servants, Kayemba sent for the fleet and set sail for Buganda. He left, however, an old and trusted chief called Namakobe in Buvuma to watch over his possessions.

Sailing from Buvuma, he spent one night at Kigombe, another at Mpirivuma, the next at Lwerwe, the next at Buto and finally one at Bukoto. When he reached Bukoto, he found no signs of mourning at all. People were making merry, drinking, and beating drums. The women, too, were cultivating their gardens. Kayemba was furious with Mulwana; so much so that he beat him till he had broken every bone in his body. When Mulwana's men saw their master being beaten to death, they sent word to the king that his brother was "killing his prime minister." The king acted promptly and sent a serious warning to Kayemba that, unless he wanted to begin hostilities, he must carry the prime minister to the capital forthwith. He added further that, if Kayemba chose to start a conflict, he was not afraid, as the royal armies were ready. Kayemba was in a dilemma. He could no longer return to Buvuma, and he was not prepared to fight, as his forces were now scattered. He therefore complied with his brother's wishes and carried Mulwana to the capital. After Bukoto, he slept at Kibibi in Kawoko, and on the following day reached Bujuko.

When Kayemba reached the capital he was reproached by the king for killing Mulwana, and also for rebelling. Kayemba defended himself, and pointed out that he was not a rebel. The reason that he had not returned after the Buvuma war was that the king was always plotting to kill him. He reminded the king of the attempt to drown him in the clay canoe. Having escaped that time, he had determined not to give the king another chance to wreak vengeance on him. After Prince Kayemba had pleaded his case, his brother did not molest him again. Instead, he commanded him to return to his former estate at Bujumba. King Juko showed this clemency because he and Kayemba were brothers of the same father and mother. In fact, they always thought of themselves as twins. The official names of their palaces were the same and their twins[7] were given the same names. Were it not for the love of power and

[7] The umbilical cord of kings and princes was preserved. It was known as the "Twin" and an official name given to it.

the jealousy that it breeds, these two brothers would have been very fond of each other.

While Kayemba was on his estate at Bujumba, Kawumpuli, his son, made him ill. Kayemba sent for both the child and his mother from Bulondoganyi. Then Kayemba, probably because he was afraid of taking a deformed child into his house, ordered some of his servants to lay the child in a small bush. Kayemba planted a tree which he called Batendagaya, in the place where the child was laid. One day, after the baby had been in the bush for some time, some medicine men came and told Kayemba that, if he wanted to succeed to the throne quickly, he must build a temple for his deformed son. They added that if ever his brother the king looked in the direction of the temple, the king would die immediately. Kayemba carried out the instructions of the medicine men at once, built a temple for his son, thatched it with a type of grass called *kukku,* and then put his child in it.

One day when the king was at his capital, some medicine men came to him and warned him that he must never look in the direction of Bulemezi, which is where Kawumpuli's temple was. They said that if the king looked in that direction he would die suddenly. They advised him to have his head covered with bark-cloth, by Nalugga, his chief wife, whenever he left the palace. In this way he could not look towards Bulemezi. Nalugga, the chief wife, always did this until she caught an eye disease which kept her indoors. The result was that there was nobody to hold a bark-cloth over the king's head when he went outside. It was then that King Juko looked in the direction of Bulemezi. When he returned to the palace he had a severe nosebleed, was overcome by dizziness, and died immediately. Everybody knew that the king's sudden death was caused by Kawumpuli, Kayemba's son. Henceforth every sudden death, or death from swollen glands in the neck and armpits, is attributed to Kawumpuli.

King Juko's body was buried at Gombe, while his jawbone was removed, taken to his capital at Bujuko, and stored in a wooden bowl.

21 / A NAVAL BATTLE ON LAKE VICTORIA IN 1875

In 1875, while on his great crossing of Africa from east to west, Sir Henry Morton Stanley was a guest of Kabaka Mutesa I of Buganda, then the dominant power in the lake regions of East Africa. He accompanied his host on a military campaign against the people of the island of Buvuma, who had refused to pay their tribute. Buvuma guards the entrance to the channel leading from Lake Victoria to the exit of the Nile. The actual scene of the lengthy naval battle was off Nakaranga Point in Busoga, a country neighboring on Buganda. Within Busoga there were a number of small states, some of them tributary to Mutesa, which had also refused to pay their tribute. The Bavuma had based themselves on Ingira, a small island between Buvuma and the mainland. Stanley estimated the number in the different Buganda army groups that made their camps at or around Nakaranga Point on September 1st as 150,000. In addition there were 50,000 women, and as many children and slaves of both sexes. The Buganda fleet numbered 325 canoes of all sizes, of which 230 were effective war vessels. The following extracts are taken from Stanley's journal.

The largest canoe seen by me in this fleet measured 72 feet in length, 7 feet, three inches in breadth, and was four feet deep within from keel to gunwale. The thwarts were 32 in number, to seat 64 paddlers beside the pilot. There were probably over 100 canoes between 50 and 70 feet in length; the remaining 80 fighting boats were of all sizes, from 18 to 30 feet long. The rest of the fleet consisted of small boats fit only to carry from three to six men.

The largest class—100 in number—would require on an average fifty men each to man them, which would be equal in the aggregate to 5000. The second class would require on an average forty men each, or two thousand to man the fifty canoes. The third class would average twenty men each, and being eighty in number, would require 1600 men to man them, the sum total standing therefore at 8600.

A very respectable figure for a naval force, most men would think. But in a battle on the lake, or for such an occasion as the present,

From H. M. Stanley, *Through the Dark Continent* (London), 1899), Vol. I, chap. xii, p. 246; chap. xiii, pp. 256-61.

when the resources of the empire were mustered for an important war, they would be further required to carry a strong force to assault Ingira Island. The canoes for the assault would therefore be crammed with fighting men, the largest class carrying from 60 to 100 men, exclusive of their crews; so that the actual fact is that Mutesa can float a force of from 16,000 to 20,000 on Lake Victoria for purposes of war.

On the fourteenth of September the Emperor of Uganda decided to give battle to the Bavuma, who were daily becoming bolder and more boastful. In the morning, in accordance with Mutesa's orders, forty Baganda canoes sallied out from the beach in front of our camps to Nakaranga Point, where they formed in line of battle before the causeway, with the sterns of their canoes fronting Ingira, and their bows toward Nakaranga Point.

Mutesa was followed by about three-fourths of his army when he proceeded to the point to view the battle, and with him went the great war drums, to the number of fifty or thereabout, and fifes about a hundred, and a great number of men shaking gourds filled with pebbles, and the court criers and mad charmers against evil were not wanting to create a din and noise, and celebrate victory.

A hut of ample size had been erected on the mountain slope overlooking the strait, into which Mutesa and his favorite women retired. When the Emperor was seated, the "prophets of Baal," or the priests and priestesses of the *Muzimu* or witchcraft, came up, more than a hundred in number, and offered the charms to Mutesa one after another in a most tedious, ceremonious way, and to all of them Mutesa condescended to point his imperial forefinger.

The chief priest was a most fantastically dressed madman. It is customary, before commencing a battle, to carry all the potent medicines or charms of Buganda (thus propitiating the dreadful *muzimu*, or evil spirits) to the monarch, that he may touch or point his forefinger at them. They consist of dead lizards, bits of wood, hide, nails of dead people, claws of animals, and beaks of birds— a hideous miscellany, with mysterious compounds of herbs and leaves carefully enclosed in vessels ornamented with vari-colored beads.

During the battle these wizards and witches chant their incantations, and exhibit their medicines on high before the foe, while the gourd and pebble bearers sound a hideous alarm, enough to cause the nerves of any man except an African to relax at once.

Mutesa and his army were in full warpaint, and the principal men wore splendid leopard skins over their backs, but the Basoga bore the palm for splendor of dress and ornate equipments.

Ankori,[1] the chief, and his officers were wonderfully gay. Snow white ostrich plumes decorated their heads, and lions and leopard skins covered their backs, while their loins were girded with snow white, long haired monkey and goat skins; even the staves of their lances were ornamented with feathers and rings of white monkey skin.

There was ample time afforded to observe all these things, and to be exceedingly amused and interested in what promised to be an animating scene, before all attention was drawn to and engaged by the battle. The spectators were seated, safe from harm or danger, on the slope of Nakaranga mountain, from the water's edge to the mountain summit, tier above tier, and rank above rank, in thousands upon thousands.

The canoes, having formed line, slowly moved sternwise toward Ingira. The Bavuma were not inactive spectators of this maneuver, but as yet their warriors had not embarked. They were busy mustering, while those appointed to garrison the island, with the women and children, several thousands in number, sat down on the slopes of the opposite mountain of Ingira Island. The rushes and weeds lining the water's edge were too tall and thick to enable us to estimate exactly the number of the enemy's war canoes, but the brown colored prows, long and curving, of a great many were seen thrust out from among the vivid green banana plantations, or arranged on the rising beach of the island beyond its reedy margin.

Having advanced with the utmost regularity of line near enough to the island to make their "Brown Bess" muskets effective, the Baganda began to open fire in a steady, deliberate manner, and succeeded after a while in annoying the foe and arousing him to action. At a given signal from their chiefs, forth from the reeds and rushes shot the prows of the Bavuma canoes; and then, giving utterance to most shrill war cries, the rowers impelled them from all quarters, to the number of 194 with an extraordinary velocity upon the

[1] The chief of those Basoga warriors who were loyal to Mutesa.

Baganda line, which now began to retire slowly toward the cause-way.[2]

On the causeway at its farthest extremity were assembled a force of a hundred musketeers and four small boat howitzers under the command of the *katikiro*[3] and Mutesa's factotum, Tori.

The furious advance of the Bavuma soon caused the Baganda to hurry their movements, and on approaching the causeway they parted their line, rushing on either side of it, giving the *katikiro* and Tori ample opportunity to wreak their will on the pursuers. But owing to the want of skill of the cannoneers, and nervousness of the musketeers, very little damage was inflicted on the Bavuma, but the noise and whirring of lead and iron sufficed to check them, and caused them to withdraw with much of the baffled aspect of hungry crocodiles cheated of their prey. This was all the battle— but short as it was, it had sufficed to prove to me that Mutesa would be unable to take Ingira Island, garrisoned and defended as it was by such a determined foe. After a while Mutesa withdrew from the scene, the army returned to its quarters, and the canoes of the Baganda, closely hugging the Nakaranga shore, went back to their rendezvous, leaving the Bavuma masters of the situation.

During the afternoon of this day Mutesa held a grand levee, and when all were assembled, he addressed them publicly to the effect that in a few days another battle would be fought. . . .

SEPTEMBER 18. Suddenly on the eighteenth of September, at early dawn, orders were communicated to the chiefs to prepare for bat-tle. The first intelligence of it that I received was from the huge war drums which summoned both sailors and warriors to action.

[*A council of war, which Stanley did not attend, was then held. Mutesa delivered a passionate speech, calling for bravery and threatening to punish any cowards. The chiefs all prostrated them-selves and swore to be desperately brave.*]

About 8:30 A.M. while I was at the point of Nakaranga, the sound of drums approached me, and I knew that the council was ended, and that the battle would soon begin. . . .

Presently other drums sounded from the waterside, and soon

---

[2] An abortive attempt had been made to construct a causeway of stones and branches, which would give access to Ingira to the Buganda land forces.

[3] Prime Minister of Buganda.

the beautiful canoes of Buganda appeared in view. The entire war-fleet of 230 vessels rode gracefully on the calm grey waters of the channel.

The line of battle, I observed, was formed by Chambarango, in command of the right flank, with fifty canoes; Sambuzi, Mukavya, Chikwata, and Saruti, all sub-chiefs, were ranged with 100 canoes under the command of Kauta, the imperial steward, to form the center; the left flank was in charge of the gallant Mkwenda,[4] who had eighty canoes. Tori commanded a force of musketeers, and with his four howitzers was stationed on the causeway, which was by this time 200 yards from the shore.

In the above manner, the fleet of vessels, containing some 16,000 men, moved to the attack on Ingira. The center, defended by the flanks which were to menace the rear of the Bavuma should they approach near the causeway, resolutely advanced to within thirty yards of Ingira, and poured in a most murderous fire among the slingers of the island, who, imagining that the Baganda meant to carry the island by storm, boldly stood exposed, resolved to fight. But they were unable to maintain that courageous behavior long. Mkwenda then moved up from the left, and attacked with his musketeers the Bavuma on the right, riddling their canoes, and making matters specially hot for them in that quarter.

The Bavuma, seeing matters approaching a crisis, and not wishing to die tamely, manned their canoes, and 196 dashed impetuously, as at first, from the rushes of Ingira with loud shrill yells, and the Baganda lines moved backward to the center of the channel, where they bravely and coolly maintained their position. As the center of the Buganda line parted in front of the causeway and disclosed the hotly advancing enemy, Tori aimed the howitzers and fired at a group of about twenty canoes, completely shattering more than half of them, and reloading quickly, he discharged several bolts of iron three inches long among them with terrible effect. Before this cool bearing of the Baganda, the Bavuma retired to their island again, and we saw numbers of canoes discharging their dead and wounded, and the Baganda were summoned to Nakaranga shore to receive the congratulations of the emperor and the applause of the vast multitude. Mutesa went down to the water's edge to express his satisfaction at their behavior.

[4] A general.

"Go at them again," said he, "and show them what fighting is." And the line of battle was again formed, and again the Bavuma darted from the cover of the reeds and water cane, with the swiftness of hungry sharks, beating the water into foam with their paddles, and rending the air with their piercing yells. It was one of the most exciting and animating scenes I ever beheld; but, owing to the terror of the stake with which their dread monarch had threatened them, the Baganda distinguished themselves for coolness and method, and the Bavuma, as on a former occasion, for intrepidity and desperate courage.

[*On two other days there were great canoe engagements, and the fortunes of war swung from side to side. Finally, Stanley claims to have brought the battle to an end by a variation on a Trojan device. An immense floating fortress was constructed under his direction, and the Bavuma were frightened into submission.*]

22 / THE VILLAGE LIFE OF EAST AFRICA

In 1858 two English explorers, Sir Richard Burton (whose account of a visit to Dahomey is given in extract 12) and John Hanning Speke, reached Lake Tanganyika. The description of village life in East Africa is taken from Burton's journal of this journey.

The assertion may startle the reader's preconceived opinions concerning the savage state of Central Africa and the wretched condition of the slave races, Negroid and Negro; but it is not less true that the African is in these regions superior in comforts, better dressed, fed, and lodged, and less worked than the unhappy Ryot of British India. His condition, where the slave trade is slack, may, indeed, be compared advantageously with that of the peasantry in some of the richest of European countries.

The African rises with the dawn from his couch of cowhide. The hut is cool and comfortable during the day, but the barred door impeding ventilation at night causes it to be close and disagreeable. The hour before sunrise being the coldest time, he usually kindles a fire, and addresses himself to his constant companion, the pipe. When the sun becomes sufficiently powerful, he removes the reed

From Richard Burton, *The Lake Regions of Central Africa* (London, 1961), Vol. II, pp. 278-79, 289.

screen from the entrance, and issues forth to bask in the morning beams. The villages are populous, and the houses touching one another enable the occupants, when squatting outside and fronting the central square, to chat and chatter without moving. About 7 A.M., when the dew has partially disappeared from the grass, the elder boys drive the flocks and herds to pasture with loud shouts and sound applications of the quarter-staff. They return only when the sun is sinking behind the western horizon. At 8 P.M. those who have provisions at home enter the hut for refection with *ugali* or holcus-porridge; those who have not, join a friend. *Pombe*,[1] when procurable, is drunk from the earliest dawn.

After breaking his fast the African repairs, pipe in hand, to the *iwanza*, the village "public," previously described. Here, in the society of his own sex, he will spend the greater part of the day talking and laughing, smoking, or torpid with sleep. Occasionally he sits down to play.

[*A description of East African games, food, alcohol, and so on, follows.*]

After eating, the East African invariably indulges in a long fit of torpidity, from which he awakes to pass the afternoon as he did the forenoon, chatting, playing, smoking, and chewing "sweet-earth." Toward sunset all issue forth to enjoy the coolness: the men sit outside the *iwanza*, whilst the women and the girls, after fetching water for household wants from the well, collecting in a group upon their little stools, indulge in the pleasures of gossipred and the pipe. This hour in the most favored parts of the country is replete with enjoyment, which even the barbarian feels, though not yet indoctrinated into aesthetics. As the hours of darkness draw nigh, the village doors are carefully closed, and, after milking his cows, each peasant retires to his hut, or passes his time with his friends in the *iwanza*.

23 / PORTRAIT OF THE GENTLE KING RUMANIKA OF KARAGWE

John Hanning Speke, after discovering Lake Tanganyika with Burton in 1858, returned to East Africa to pursue his quest for

---

[1] Beer.

the Nile's sources. In 1863 he arrived at Karagwe, a small state to the west of Lake Victoria. Speke—and Stanley[1] when he came there in 1876—found an especially sympathetic friend in King Rumanika. The rulers of Karagwe, like those of Ankole,[2] were Bahima. It was the first time that either Speke or Burton had met any of the peoples of mixed Caucasian and Negroid features, sometimes referred to as Hamitic peoples, on the assumption that they came originally from an area where Hamitic languages are spoken. More than five hundred years ago they trickled over Africa, settling down in pastoral communities and dominating majority populations of Negro agriculturalists.

Speke's Description

To do royal honors to the king of this charming land, I ordered my men to put down their loads and fire a volley. This was no sooner done than, as we went to the palace gate, we received an invitation to come in at once, for the king wished to see us before attending to anything else. Now, leaving our traps outside, both Grant[1] and myself, attended by Bombay and a few of the seniors of my Banguana,[2] entered the vestibule, and, walking through extensive enclosures studded with huts of kingly dimensions, were escorted to a pent-roofed *baraza*,[3] which the Arabs had built as a sort of government office, where the king might conduct his state affairs.

Here, as we entered, we saw sitting cross-legged on the ground Rumanika the King, and his brother Nnanaji, both of them men of noble appearance and size. The king was plainly dressed in an Arab's black *choga*, and wore, for ornament, dress stockings of rich colored beads, and neatly worked wristlets of copper. Nnanaji, being a doctor of very high pretensions, in addition to a check cloth wrapped round him, was covered with charms. At their sides lay huge pipes of black clay. In their rear, squatting quiet as mice, were all the king's sons, some six or seven lads, who wore leather

From John Hanning Speke, *Journal of the Discovery of the Source of the Nile* (London, 1863), pp. 202-206.

[1] See extract 21.
[2] See extract 25.
[1] Speke's companion.
[2] Speke's porters were Banguana, or coastal people.
[3] Verandah or porch.

middle-coverings, and little dream charms tied under their chins. The first greetings of the king, delivered in good Kiswahili, were warm and affecting, and in an instant we both felt and saw we were in the company of men who were as unlike as they could be to the common order of natives of the surrounding districts. They had fine oval faces, large eyes, and high noses, denoting the best blood of Abyssinia. Having shaken hands in true English style, which is the peculiar custom of the men of this country, the ever-smiling Rumanika begged us to be seated on the ground opposite to him, and at once wished to know what we thought of Karagwe, for it had struck him his mountains were the finest in the world; and the lake, too—did we not admire it?

[*Speke then recounts some of his adventures on his journey from the coast.*]

Time flew like magic, the king's mind was so quick and inquiring; but as the day was wasting away, he generously gave us our option to choose a place for our residence in or out of his palace, and allowed us time to select one. We found the view overlooking the lake to be so charming that we preferred camping outside, and set our men at once to work cutting sticks and long grass to erect themselves sheds.

One of the young princes—for the king ordered them all to be constantly in attendance on us—happening to see me sit in an iron chair, rushed back to his father and told him about it. This set all the royals in the palace in a state of high wonder, and ended by my getting a summons to show off the white man sitting on his throne; for of course I could only be, as all of them called me, a king of great dignity, to indulge in such state. Rather reluctantly I did as I was bid, and allowed myself once more to be dragged into court. Rumanika, as gentle as ever, then burst into a fresh fit of merriment, and, after making sundry enlightened remarks of inquiry, which of course were responded to with the greatest satisfaction, finished off by saying, with a very expressive shake of the head, "Oh, these Basungu,[4] these Basungu! they know and do everything."

I then put in a word for myself. Since we had entered Karagwe we never could get one drop of milk either for love or money, and

[4] White men.

I wished to know what motive the Bahima had for withholding it. We had heard they held superstitious dreads; that any one who ate the flesh of pigs, fish, or fowl, or the bean called *maharagwe,* if he tasted the products of their cows, would destroy their cattle—and I hoped he did not labor under any such absurd delusions. To which he replied, it was only the poor who thought so; and as he now saw we were in want, he would set apart one of his cows expressly for our use. On bidding adieu, the usual formalities of hand-shaking were gone through; and on entering camp, I found the good thoughtful king had sent us some more of his excellent beer.

Stanley's Description

On the grassy terrace below us was situated Rumanika's village, fenced round by a strong and circular stockade, to which we now descended after having enjoyed a noble and inspiring prospect.

Our procession was not long in attracting hundreds of persons, principally youths—all those who might be considered in their boyhood being perfectly nude.

"Who are these?" I inquired of Shaikh Hamed.[1]

"Some of the youngsters are sons of Rumanika, others are young Banya-Rwanda," [2] he replied.

The sons of Rumanika, nourished on a milk diet, were in remarkably good condition. Their unctuous skins shone as though the tissues of fat beneath were dissolving in the heat, and their rounded bodies were as taut as a drum head. Their eyes were large, and beaming and lustrous with life, yet softened by an extreme gentleness of expression. The sculptor might have obtained from any of these royal boys a dark model for another statue to rival the classic Antinous.

As we were followed by the youths, who welcomed us with a graceful courtesy, the appropriate couplet came to my mind—

> Thrice happy race! that innocent of blood,
> From milk innoxious, seek their simple food.

We were soon ushered into the hut where Rumanika sat ex-

From H. M. Stanley, *Through the Dark Continent* (London, 1899), Vol. I, chap. xvii, pp. 358-359.

[1] An Arab merchant residing in Karagwe.
[2] People of Rwanda. See below, extract 26.

pectant, with one of the kindliest, most paternal smiles it would be possible to conceive.

I confess to have been as affected by the first glance at this venerable and gentle pagan as though I gazed on the serene and placid face of some Christian patriarch or saint of old, whose memory the church still holds in reverence. His face reminded me of a deep still well; the tones of his voice were so calm that unconsciously they compelled me to imitate him. . . .

24 / THE FATTENED PRINCESSES OF KARAGWE

NOV. 26, 1881. In the afternoon, as I had heard from Musa that the wives of the kings and princes were fattened to such an extent that they could not stand upright, I paid my respects to Wazezeru, the king's eldest brother—who, having been born before his father ascended his throne, did not come in the line of succession—with the hope of being able to see for myself the truth of the story. There was no mistake about it. On entering the hut I found the old man and his chief wife sitting side by side on a bench of earth strewed over with grass, and partitioned like stalls for sleeping apartments, whilst in front of them were placed numerous wooden pots of milk, and, hanging from the poles that supported the beehive shaped hut, a large collection of bows six feet in length, whilst below them were tied an even larger collection of spears, intermixed with a goodly assortment of heavy-handed assegais.[1] I was struck with no small surprise at the way he received me, as well as with the extraordinary dimensions, yet pleasing beauty, of the immoderately fat fair one, his wife. She could not rise; and so large were her arms that, between the joints the flesh hung down like large, loose-stuffed puddings. Then in came their children, all models of the Abyssinian type of beauty, and as polite in their manners as thoroughbred gentlemen. They had heard of my picture-books from the king, and all wished to see them; which they no sooner did, to their infinite delight, especially when they recognized any of the animals, than the subject was turned by my inquiring what they did with

From John Hanning Speke, *Journal of the Discovery of the Source of the Nile* (London, 1863), pp. 209-210, 231.

[1] Spears made of hard wood.

so many milk pots. This was easily explained by Wazezeru himself, who, pointing to his wife, said, "This is all the product of those pots: from early youth upward we keep those pots to their mouths, as it is the fashion at court to have very fat wives."

[*Three weeks later, while still staying with Rumanika, Speke went to get the measurements of another large lady.*]

DECEMBER 14, 1861. After a long and amusing conversation with Rumanika in the morning, I called on one of his sisters-in-law, married to an elder brother who was born before Dagara ascended the throne. She was another of those wonders of obesity, unable to stand excepting on all fours. I was desirous to obtain a good view of her, and induced her to give me facilities for doing so, by offering in return to show her a bit of my naked legs and arms. The bait took as I wished it, and, after getting her to sidle and wriggle into the middle of the hut, I did as I promised, and then took her dimensions, as noted below.[2] All of these are exact except the height, and I believe I could have obtained this more accurately if I could have had her laid on the floor. Not knowing what difficulties I should have to contend with in such a piece of engineering, I tried to get her height by raising her up. This, after infinite exertions on the part of us both, was accomplished, when she sank down again, fainting, for her blood had rushed into her head. Meanwhile, the daughter, a lass of sixteen, sat stark naked before us, sucking at a milk pot, on which the father kept her at work by holding a rod in his hand, for as fattening is the first duty of fashionable female life, it must be duly enforced by the rod if necessary. I got up a bit of flirtation with missy, and induced her to rise and shake hands with me. Her features were lovely, but her body was as round as a ball.

25 / HEROIC POETRY OF ANKOLE

Ankole in western Uganda is the principal home of the Bahima.[1] *Though only a small minority in the population, they were the rulers of the country for many centuries. They are famous for their*

[2] Round arm, 1 ft. 11 in.; chest, 4 ft. 4 in.; thigh, 2 ft. 7 in.; calf, 1 ft. 8 in.; height, 5 ft. 8 in.

[1] See extract 23.

*herds of beautiful long-horned cattle, which form an integral part
of their social structure. They have their own form of poetic art—
metric recitations which are essentially individual compositions.
They are recited in the evening, when the cattle are gathered into
the kraals. Formerly, every Muhima was expected to cultivate this
art which now only survives among the uneducated herdsmen. Many
of them become great artists, both in composition and in performance.*

*Although there is considerable elasticity in the length of line
and verse, there are definite structural conventions in this poetry.
A whole verse is recited at tremendous speed, without taking breath,
by the performer, who stands, sometimes with his arm extended to
his spear which is stuck in the ground, and sometimes with the
spear poised on high, using rapid forward thrusts to emphasize
dramatically the points of interest.*

*In subject matter the recitations are of two kinds: those that
boast of the author's military prowess, and those that extol the
beauty of his herd. The poem given here is of the latter kind, and
tells the story of one of the herds—the Abatangaaza, or "Marvelous
Ones"—belonging to the Omugabe, or king.*

*After an introductory description of the herd, it goes on to tell
of the sufferings of the cattle during a devastating outbreak of
rinderpest which occurred in the second decade of this century.
Pasturing far afield at the time, the depleted herd continued to
suffer as it searched desperately for water on the long journey homeward. Their beauty was restored when they finally found water.*

*The proper names of both persons and cows are replaced by
praise-names, such as "The One Whose Horns Are Well Spread."
Despite the great number of place names which make it rather difficult to read, the poetry and the pathos are readily discernible.*

The Marvelous Ones

At Katunguru near Rurangizi, *She Who Teases* lay back her horns
  and so did *She Who Approaches the Fighters;*
At Kahama near Kambarango, we deceived *The One Who Drives
  Back The Others* with the calf of *The One Whose Horns Are
  Well Spread* pretending it were hers.[1]

From H. F. Morris, *The Heroic Recitations of Bahima of Ankole* (Oxford: The
Clarendon Press, 1964), pp. 104-112. Reprinted by permission of The Clarendon
Press.

[1] The cow had lost her calf, and was shown another calf to persuade her to
give her milk.

At Rwenfukuzi near Ndeego, the lazy ones of Migina marveled at the white patch of the daughter of *The One With The Blaze On Her Forehead* as she gamboled;

At Kabura and Nyansheko, they marveled at the horns of the strawberry beast of Rwatikungu, *She Whose Horns Are Not Stunted.*

At Kiyegayega near Migina, the varied herd made a noise as they went to Rusheesa;

At Rwekubo near Kinanga, the herd walked proudly having killed a loaned beast.

She Whose Horns Stand Out Above The Herd gave birth and so did *She Who Has Straightened Her Horns;*

She Who Prevents Others Approaching became friendly with *The One Whose Horns Are Straight As Planks.*

At Akabaare at Nyamukondo's, they prepared their camps;
At Igwanjura and Wabinyonyi, they had slim bodies.[2]

At Byembogo, they played with the antelopes;
At Ntarama, they borrowed the dress of the sorcerers;[3]
At Kakono near Rubaya, we gave them another bell when they refused to increase.[4]

At Shagama and Rwabigyemano, they displayed the tips of their horns;
At Bunonko in Rwanda,[5] they danced about and played in the light rain;
At Nsikizi in Rwanda, they prevented the bell of *The Leader* from ringing.

At Burungu at the home of *The One Who Is Not Dissuaded From Fighting,*[6]
At Rwoma and Ihondaniro, they returned facing Kaaro;

[2] Slimness in a cow is considered a point of beauty.
[3] The cattle in the herd were red, white, and brown, which were the colors of the dresses worn by the oracle diviners.
[4] The herd was divided in the hope that the cattle would increase.
[5] Rwanda in Ankole, not the country called Rwanda.
[6] Praise-name of a person, not a cow.

At Nyumba and Rwemiganda, they were patient in death;

At Obukomago and Nyambindo, they died as the princes died in Buganda;[7]

Alas! I am heartbroken at the groaning of *The One Who Returns Home With Pride*.

At Katebe and Muzaire, blue-fly[8] put on his boots;

At Rwomugina and Rwobusisi, he found them grazing at the noontide;

That was when they amazed the Bagina[9] of Ntuugu near Mugore,

Who asked whether *She Whose Horns Reach Across The Watering Troughs* and *She Whose Horns Are Like Polished Reeds* were produced by the daughter of *The One Whose Horns Penetrate The Bushes*.

I replied: "You do not know them at all;

Are they not the progeny of the daughter of *The Leader Who Makes The Counties Stand Still In Admiration?*"

Or what about when they amazed the Muganda of Burunga,[10]

Who asked if *She Who Grazes On The Ridge* and *She Who Fears Disease*, who were so friendly, were of one mother?

I replied: "If they are not known by us who are their owners, how can they be known by the hangers-on of Europeans?"[11]

At Endongo near Bwarukuba, they grazed while they were feverish;

At Rugushuru near Mirekaano, they brought me into a land recently scorched by the sun.

At Buteeteera near Butuntunuura, at Kenshunga near Nyina-ibaare,

At Rwomunago near Rwakasheegu, at Rwenkombero near Kyaburatsi,

---

[7] This refers to a massacre.

[8] I.e., the bluebottle fly, preparing to buzz around the cattle's corpses. Uganda's policemen wore blue jerseys and boots; they, too, were apt to buzz around corpses. This sort of telescoped imagery is usual in this poetry.

[9] An Ankole clan amazed at the beauty of the cattle.

[10] A chief.

[11] Those who have abandoned Bahima customs for European ways.

At Maka-abiri near Rubirizi, at Mukora-iguru near Garumuri,
they pressed me like challenging warriors.[12]

At Rushoga and Bigango, at Kagaaga near Binda, the fight was
started
By *The Black And Red One*, daughter of *The One Who Stays
Still* and by her sister, *She Who Gives Blows And Bruises;*
The newly burnt land was too much for the daughter of *The
Brown One;* they told me of Obwiha and Mushaija;
I replied that they troubled me by suggesting a return to Kama-
tungu.

All at Mukande, the heedless ones wished to struggle at the
water trough,
The Breaker, the tawny cow of Kaniaga and *The Leader,* the
brown cow of *The Mender Of Broken Bones;*[13]
The Swift One gamboled at Buyonza,
Her horns disappeared from the sight of the proud.[14]

I said: *"She Who Lifts Up Her Horns Brown As The Enkuraijo
Tree* and the granddaughter of *The Strawberry One* have slept
without water; I have gone to and fro with *The One Free From
Disease";*
They pleased those who met them having come from Obuyonza
and drunk water on the way to Emiriti[15];
She Whose Horns Are For No Mere Display[16] ran as they returned
home; the milkers avoiding *The Restless One;*
The slim cows of Rwaburaga had horns pointing upward.

26 / DYNASTIC POETRY OF RWANDA

*The kingdom of Rwanda, like Ankole, was ruled for many cen-
turies by a minority of pastoralists, in this case the Batutsi, distant*

From Alexis Kagame, *La Poésie dynastique de Ruanda* (Brussels: IRCB Publication, 1951), pp. 10-11.

[12] They were suffering from thirst.
[13] The praise-name of an Omugabe.
[14] Those cheeky enough to think they could touch the tips of the horns.
[15] Having found water their beauty was restored.
[16] She used them to fight with.

cousins of the Bahima.[1] *Much of their great wealth of traditional poetry has been recorded. It is of three kinds: pastoral poetry, war poetry, and dynastic poetry. The latter was devoted to the praise of the king and the reigning house. The following piece is a translation from a French version by the Abbé Alexis Kagame, a munyarwanda priest. The poem was composed in 1875 by a court bard, on the occasion of a successful punitive expedition against the island of Ijwi in Lake Kivu, whose petty king had refused to pay tribute to King Gigele IV of Rwanda.*

As God has given us an occasion for rejoicing,
I take the opportunity to sing the praises of the kings. . . .
Oh! you Basindi! [2] God gave you a sacred fertility,
So that you should become strong and should reign without frontier,
And be raised up above your rivals!
Oh princes of happy omen, you are the rulers!
You have a profound peace,
So that great renown has become your attribute. . . .

Oh guardian of life, I acclaim your triumphs,[3]
And your continuity.
You have put down foreign kings,
Beyond all comparison you are their superior.
You possess, more than all of them the God that chose you,
Who gave you success, making you to triumph over the foreigner.
He has preserved to you the succession and the royal possessions.[4]

And when you attack, you never retire vanquished. . . .
Thou hast exterminated the murderers of thy family,
Thou hast annihilated the descendants of Ntsibura,[5]
They are vanquished never to return!

[1] See extract 25.

[2] The reigning dynasty of Rwanda.

[3] The bard sometimes addresses the whole line of Basindi kings, and sometimes the reigning king; hence the recurring changes between the singular and plural person.

[4] Literally the "royal spouses." The king was proclaimed the "husband" of each new conquest.

[5] The warrior Ntsibura, the eponymous ancestor of the dynasty ruling in Ijwi, had killed a king of Rwanda in the sixteenth century.

Since thy succession victories are unending;

Thou hast saved us from innumerable calamities. . . .

Dost thou know, oh unsurpassable! what made thee superior to thine enemies?

Thou excellest in the skill that triumphs over treason.

When we urge thee to battle, thou fightest like a strong bull.

Being unafraid of the deep waters, thou didst pass beneath them,

Which caused terrible confusion in the Ijwi;

And the avenger's javelin gained unforgettable renown for us there,

In the Marambo as well as the Nyakarengo.[6]

The people know thee no more by name, having seen thee with their own eyes,

When the fires mingled with the dolorous death cries!

And so successful voyager,

Thy marches have become devastating!

Is it true that thou didst depart without a signal for mobilization,

That thou didst take the road as though for an afternoon walk,

Letting it be thought that thou wast visiting the capitals of thy fathers? [7]

Once across the mountain region thou didst change direction

And gave the army the order to attack!

Thou didst take an impassable road, oh hero chief of the armies!

And traversed Lake Kivu as though it were a bowl of water!

Thy javelin brought about a terrible carnage amongst the islanders!

They were exterminated in bewildered astonishment,

Saying they were the victims of an attack by the king of the firmament.[8] . . .

27 / THE COURT OF THE CHRISTIAN KINGDOM OF CONGO IN THE SIXTEENTH CENTURY

The kingdom of Congo, to the south of the Congo river estuary, was converted to Christianity by Portuguese priests in 1491, and

From Duarte Lopez and Filipo Pigafetta, *Relação do Reino de Congo* (a reprint of the original Italian) (Lisbon, 19–?), Book II, chap. VII, pp. 66-69.

[6] Places in Ijwi.

[7] Each king moved his capital from time to time, but a capital once founded, became "espoused" to the royal house forever.

[8] I.e., of thunder and lightning.

remained in contact with western Christendom for nearly two hundred years. Duarte Lopez, a Portuguese Jewish convert, arrived at the capital, San Salvador, at the end of 1578 or the beginning of 1579, in the reign of Alvaro I, the sixth king of the Christian era. Lopez established himself as a respected merchant, evidently dealing principally in slaves. He gained the confidence of the king who made him a "fidalgo," or gentleman of his household.

In 1583, Alvaro appointed Lopez as his ambassador on a mission to Spain and the Holy See. The king was greatly worried at the time by the deterioration of Christianity in his realm—a result of both the scarcity and the poor quality of the Portuguese priests. Lopez went with secret instructions for negotiating a transfer of Congo from the tutelage of Portugal to direct obedience to the Holy See. (His official instructions, dated January 15, 1583, are still extant in various translations.) In the summer of 1588, having traveled through Portugal and Spain, he arrived at Rome, where he was taken under the wing of Monsignor Migliore, coadjutor to Cardinal Montalfo. It was probably Migliore who presented Lopez to Pope Sixtus V, and it was certainly he who asked the humanist, writer, traveler, and geographer, Filipo Pigafetta, to contact Lopez in order to extract from him the information necessary for a complete description of Congo. They had many meetings in the second half of 1588 and in 1589. From these meetings, and from some writings of Lopez, not known to exist today, resulted La Relazione del reame di Congo. *The extract that follows contains some descriptions of the king's court, with its vivid mixture of African and Portuguese customs.*

In ancient times the king and his courtiers dressed themselves in cloths made from palms, as we have previously described. With these they covered the lower part of the body, securing them with a belt woven from the same material, and finely worked. In front they used to suspend, like aprons, pretty and delicate little skins of animals, such as baby tigers, civet cats, sables, and martens, always with the head left on.

To make a grander show, they used to throw a sort of circular rochet across the bare shoulders. This came down below the knees, and was made of a net of fine threads, the mesh being edged with fringed hoops, which gave a very graceful effect. This rochet was thrown back over the right shoulder, in order to leave the hand free, and on the same shoulder they used to carry a zebra tail attached to a handle, for the cult of elegance is an ancient tradition in these regions. On their heads they wore a little square crowned cap of red and yellow, that covered the top of the head, and which was more of an ornament than protection against air and sun. Most people went barefoot, but the king and some of his courtiers wore the kind of shoes one sees on classical Roman statues, and which were of the same material, made from palm fibers.

The poor and common people dressed from the waist down in the way described, but using coarser cloth. The upper part of the body was naked.

The women cover the lower part of the body with three cloths, one long and coming down to the heels, the second shorter, and the third shorter still and edged with its own fringe. Each of them are draped on the cross and open in front. They cover the breast with a bodice that comes down to the waist. The cloths are made from the same palm fibers, as are also the capes they wear on their shoulders. They go about with the face uncovered, and wearing similar little caps to the men.

Middle class women also dress in this fashion, but using coarser material. The slaves and lower class women only cover the body from the waist down, the rest being naked.

But after the kingdom had received the Christian faith, the grandees of the court began to dress like the Portuguese, wearing mantles, capes, and cloaks of scarlet silk, each according to his means. They began to wear hats, and bonnets, and velvet and leather sandals, and Portuguese style bootees, and to carry large swords at the side.

The common people who cannot afford to dress in the Portuguese fashion continue to wear the traditional costume.

The women also dress like the Portuguese, except that they do not wear the cloak. They cover their heads with a veil, and place under it a cap of black velvet ornamented with jewels, and they wear several gold chains round the neck. Only the ladies of the court adorn themselves in this fashion. The poor retain the old costumes.

When the king was converted to Christianity, he reformed the court to a certain extent in imitation of that of the king of Portugal, beginning with the service of his table. When he eats in public, they erect a three-tiered dais covered with Indian carpets. On it they place the table with a seat of crimson velvet studded with gold nails. The king always eats there alone, as no one may sit at table with him. The princes remain covered. He has table plate of gold and silver, which does credit to his food and drink. He has a guard composed of "Anzichi" [1] and of other nationalities, who hang around his palace and are equipped with the aforesaid arms. When he wishes to go out, they sound kettle drums that can be heard at a distance of five or six miles, to warn the people of his intention. All the gentlemen accompany him, as well as the Portuguese, in whom he places great confidence. But it is rarely that he leaves his palace.

It is his custom to give public audience twice a week, at which only the grandees speak. As no one in the kingdom has estates or private possessions, but everything belongs to the crown, there is no litigation. Except for a few words, writing is not used, even in the Congo language. In criminal cases punishment is light, and it is rarely that anyone is condemned to death. Misdemeanors committed by the Mocicongo (as the inhabitants of Congo call themselves in their own language) against the Portuguese, are judged according to the laws of Portugal. If a crime is committed against a Congolese, the king deports the culprit to a desert island. He deems that to exile him in this manner until he has repented of his sins is to punish him more severely than if he was dealt with at one blow. If those that have been condemned to such a punishment survive for ten or twelve years, the king always pardons them and they are people of some consideration, and even employed in the service of the state, as men who have made amends, and who are accustomed to suffering.

In civil affairs the rule is that the Portuguese who has a lawsuit against a Mocicongo presents it before a Congo judge; and that the Mocicongo who accuses a Portuguese cites it before a Portuguese who fulfills the functions of both consul and judge in this country, by permission of the king. In proceedings among themselves and with the Portuguese they use neither writing nor instruments, but deal with the cases on the oral evidence of witnesses.

Having no knowledge of writing, they do not preserve either the history of their kings or of bygone centuries. They generally

[1] The Bateke, who live to the north of the Congo.

measure time by moons, and they do not divide night and day into hours. They are in the habit of saying that it was in the time of "such and such" that "such and such" a thing happened. The distance between places is not calculated in miles or any similar measure, but by marching days, loaded or unloaded.

On their joyful festive occasions, such as marriages, they sing love-songs accompanied by lutes of a strange shape. . . .

The musicians pluck the strings of the instrument decorously, and with the fingers, without a keyboard, as the harp is played. They strike the lute with mastery, producing thus a melody or a sound—I don't know which to call it—which delights their ear. What is more (and it is an admirable thing), by means of this instrument they express their thoughts, and they make themselves so clear that almost everything that can be put into words they can render by means of the fingers touching this instrument. To it they dance a measure, clapping their hands to mark the rhythm of the music.

At the king's court there are also flutes and fifes which they play with artistry. They dance to the sound of these instruments with gravity and dignity, the foot movements resembling Moorish dancing. The common people play on kettle drums and flutes and other instruments, but in a cruder way than the courtiers.

28 / THE JAGAS

Andrew Battell, a native of Leigh in Essex, sailed from Plymouth for South America in May 1589. He was captured by the Portuguese in the River of Janeiro, and sent as a prisoner to Angola, which he reached in the summer of 1590. During many adventurous years there he traveled extensively in the interior, the first white man to do so. When he returned to England around 1610, he recounted his experiences to the Reverend Samuel Purchas, the great recorder, translator, and editor of travel memoirs, who was then Vicar of Eastwood, which is two miles from Leigh. Purchas incorporated the information acquired during many conferences with Battell in Purchas His Pilgrimage, *published in 1613. After Battell's death, his personal narrative came into Purchas's possession, and was incorporated by him into* Hakluytus Posthumus or Purchas His Pil-

Andrew Battell. From *The Strange Adventures of Andrew Battell of Leigh,* ed. E. G. Ravenstein (London: Hakluyt Society, 1901), pp. 28-35.

grimes, *published in 1625. From this narrative comes the account
of the Jagas, with whom Battell lived for sixteen months. Although
Purchas asserts that the Jagas came from Sierra Leone, Battell
clearly had no ideas on their origins. They were, in fact, a notori-
ously warlike offshoot of the Baluba,* the virile people living
around the headwaters of the Congo tributaries.*

There were in the camp of the Jagas twelve captains. The first,
called Imbe Calandola, their general, a man of great courage. He
warreth all by enchantment, and taketh the devil's counsel in all
his exploits. He is always making of sacrifices to the devil, and doth
know many times what shall happen unto him. He believeth that
he shall never die but in the wars. There is no image among them,
but he useth certain ceremonies. He hath straight laws to his soldiers: for those that are faint-hearted and turn their backs to
the enemy are presently condemned and killed for cowards, and
their bodies eaten. He useth every night to make a warlike oration
upon an high scaffold, which doth encourage his people. It is the
order of these people, wheresoever they pitch their camp, although
they stay but one night in a place, to build their fort, with such
wood or trees as the place yieldeth: so that the one part of them
cutteth down trees and boughs, and the other part carrieth them,
and buildeth a round circle with twelve gates. So that every captain keepeth his gate. In the middle of the fort is the general's
house, intrenched round about, and he hath many porters to keep
the door. They build their houses very close together, and have
their bows, arrows, and darts standing without their doors; and
when they give alarm, they are suddenly all out of the fort. Every
company at their doors keep very good watch in the night, playing
upon their drums and *tavales*.[1]

These Jagas told us of a river that is to the southward of the
Bay of Vaccas,[2] that hath great store of gold: and that they gathered
up great store of grains of gold upon the sand, which the fresh
water driveth down in the time of rain. We found some of this gold
in the handles of their hatchets, which they use to engrave with
copper; and they called it copper also, and do not esteem it.

These Jagas delight in no country, but where there is great store

* See introduction.
[1] Wooden drums.
[2] Benguella Bay.

of *palmares,* or groves of palms. For they delight greatly in the wine and in the fruit of the palm, which serveth to eat and to make oil. And they draw their wine contrary to the Imbondos.[3] These palm trees are six or seven fathoms high, and have no leaves but in the top: and they have a device to go up to the top of the tree, and lay no hands on it, and they draw the wine in the top of the tree in a bottle.

But these Jagas cut the palm tree down by the root, which lie ten days before they will give wine. And then they make a square hole in the top and heart of a tree, and take out of the hole every morning a quart, and at night a quart. So that every tree giveth two quarts of wine a day for the space of six and twenty days, and then it drieth up.

When they settle themselves in any country, they cut down as many palms as will serve them wine for a month: and then as many more, so that in a little time they spoil the country. They stay no longer in a place than it will afford them maintenance. And then in harvest time they arise, and settle themselves in the fruitfullest place they can find; and do reap their enemy's corn, and take their cattle. For they will not sow, nor plant, nor bring up any cattle, more than they take by wars. When they come into any country that is strong, which they cannot the first day conquer, then their general buildeth his fort, and remaineth sometimes a month or two quiet. For he saith, it is as great [as] wars to the inhabitants to see them settled in their country, as though he fought with them every day. So that many times the inhabitants come and assault him in his fort: and these Jagas defend themselves and flesh[4] them on for the space of two or three days. And when their general mindeth to give the onset, he will, in the night, put out some thousand men: which do ambush themselves about a mile from their fort. Then in the morning the great Jaga goeth with all his strength out of the fort, as though he would take their town. The inhabitants coming near the fort to defend their country, being between them, the Jagas give the watchword with their drums, and then the ambushed men arise, so that very few escape. And that day their general overunneth the country.

---

[3] The Mbundu of Angola, who draw the wine from the top of the standing tree.

[4] Encourage.

The great Jaga Calandola hath his hair very long, embroidered with many knots of *bamba*[5] shells, which are very rich among them, and about his neck a collar of *masoes*,[6] which are also shells that are found upon that coast, and are among them for the worth of twenty shillings a shell: and about his middle he weareth *landes*, which are beads made of ostrich eggs.[7] He weareth a palm-cloth about his middle, as fine as silk. His body is carved and cut with sundry works, and every day anointed with the fat of men. He weareth a piece of copper cross his nose, two inches long, and in his ears also. His body is always painted red and white. He hath twenty or thirty wives, which follow him when he goeth abroad; and one of them carrieth his bows and arrows; and four of them carry his cups of drink after him. And when he drinketh they all kneel down, and clap their hands and sing.

Their women wear their hair with high *trompes* full of *bamba* shells, and are anointed with civet. They pull out four of their teeth, two above and two below, for a bravery. And those that have not their teeth out are loathsome to them, and shall neither eat nor drink with them. They wear a great store of beads about their necks, arms, and legs; about their middles, silk cloths. The women are very fruitful, but they enjoy none of their children: for as soon as the woman is delivered of her child, it is presently buried quick [i.e., alive], so that there is not one child brought up in all this generation. But when they take any town they keep the boys and girls of thirteen or fourteen years of age as their own children. But the men and women they kill and eat. These little boys they train up in the wars, and hang a collar about their necks for a disgrace, which is never taken off till he proveth himself a man, and brings his enemy's head to the general: and then it is taken off and he is a freeman, and is called *gonso* or soldier. This maketh them all desperate, and forward to be free, and counted men: and so they do increase. In all this camp there were but twelve natural Jagas that were their captains, and fourteen or fifteen women. . . . But their camp is sixteen thousand strong, and sometimes more.

When the great Jaga Calandola undertaketh any great enterprise against the inhabitants of any country, he maketh a sacrifice to the

[5] Whelk or trumpet shells.

[6] Probably turritella or screw-shells.

[7] Battell, or possibly Purchas, is mistaken as there are no ostriches in Angola.

devil, in the morning, before the sun riseth. He sitteth upon a stool, having upon each side of him a man-witch: then he hath forty or fifty women which stand round about him, holding in each hand a zebra or wild horse's tail, wherewith they do flourish and sing. Behind them are great store of *petes, ponges,* and drums, which always play. In the midst of them is a great fire; upon the fire an earthen pot with white powders, wherewith the men-witches do paint him on the forehead, temples, 'thwart the breast and belly, with long ceremonies and enchanting terms. Thus he continueth till sun is down. Then the witches bring his *casengula,*[8] which is a weapon like a hatchet, and put it into his hand, and bid him be strong against his enemies: for his *mokiso*[9] is with him. And presently there is a man-child brought, which forthwith he killeth. There are four men brought before him; two whereof, as it happeneth, he presently striketh and killeth; the other two he commandeth to be killed without the fort.

Here I was by the men-witches ordered to go away, as I was a Christian, for then the devil does appear to them as they say. And repesently he commandeth five cows to be killed within the fort, and five without the fort: and likewise as many goats and as many dogs, and the blood of them is sprinkled in the fire, and their bodies eaten with great feasting and triumph. And this is used many times by all the other captains in their army.

When they bury the dead they make a vault in the ground, and a seat for him to sit. The dead hath his head newly embroidered, his body washed, and anointed with sweet powders.

29 / THE OFFICERS OF STATE OF LUNDA

In 1831 a Portuguese expedition left Tete, six hundred miles up the Zambezi, bound for Lunda, the Kingdom of Mwata Kazembe. Situated between Lakes Mweru and Bangweolo, Lunda was then a larger and more powerful state than it is today. The Portuguese, who wished to establish trading relations and to explore a possible route across the continent to Angola, accomplished neither of their

From A. C. P. Gamitto, *King Kazembe and the Marave, Cheva, Bisa, Bemba, Lunda and Other Peoples of Southern Africa.* Translated by Ian Cunnison (Lisbon, 1960), Vol. II, pp. 111-13.

[8] War hatchet.
[9] Idol.

objectives. Antonio Gamitto, second-in-command of the expedition, kept a meticulous diary in which he made interesting ethnographic notes on the Lunda, and on other peoples encountered on the journey. This work, only recently translated into English, is the earliest detailed account of that part of Africa which was directly influenced by the Luba.[1] *The superior technical skill with which the Luba mined and worked copper as early as the eight or ninth century,* A.D. *evidently led to prosperity and a population explosion. It is known from oral tradition that Luba emigrants settled down as a ruling class among both the Lunda and the Marave peoples, who are described by Gamitto in the two succeeding extracts.*

The list of officers at Kazembe's court, and the account of their functions, shows that the elaborate machinery of government which has been described elsewhere was common to all great states in Africa. The despots ruled through a hierarchy of officials which was more like a civil service than a hereditary feudal nobility.

The court of the *Mwata Kazembe* is composed of *chilolos,* or *vambires,* who constitute a nobility, and these are respected by the people in the same way as they themselves respect Kazembe. The principal *chilolos* are:

The *mwana-bute,* the heir to the throne;
The *kalulua,* uncle of the *matwa;*
The *nswanamulopwe,* nephew of the *mwata;*
The *nyina-mwana,* mother of the *mwata;*
The *nambansa,* sister of the *mwata* (these two last titles are honorary);
The *mwinempanda,* general-in-chief of the warriors;
The *mwaniansita,* intendant of the roads, with the responsibility of finding guides; he also has to hear and pronounce upon cases before they are finally judged by the mwata.

The other *chilolos,* whose titles are preceded by the word *mfumu,* belong to the second order.

All the articles of clothing and ornament of the *mwata* are under the management and care of *chilolos* of the second order; and each kind of article has its own keeper, who takes his title therefrom. Thus the *mfumwa-mukonso* keeps the *mukonso* skirt of the *mwata;* the *mfumwa-tunseko* keeps the beads; the *mfumwa-mabwe* keeps the precious stones, etc., etc.

[1] See Introduction.

These *chilolos* are obliged always to be near the *musumba*[1] where they can hear the sound of the talking drum. Besides these, there are instrument players who have the same title as the instruments they play, and who are also considered *chilolos* of the second order.

The supreme authority is that of Kazembe, and the second in power is [the] *mwinempanda,* who is commander-in-chief when all or the greater part of the nation takes up arms; the only time he does not have this position is when Kazembe himself takes command.

The *mwaniansita,* or superintendent of the roads, has the duty of preparing itineraries for caravans, of providing an escort under the command of one of his subordinates, to whom he gives instructions about the passage. The subordinate is then his representative and takes his title. He himself marches only with Kazembe.

The *mfumbwa-lubinda* is inspector of works to the *mwata,* and his duty is to repair and maintain the streets of Lunda, the fences and houses of the *musumba,* the *masembe,*[2] the *mashamos,*[3] and so on. He is subordinate to the *mwaniasita.*

The *kakwata,* whose title means literally "he who seizes and escorts" does not have the character of *chilolo;* all the same, he is a respected authority, but one who is at the same time detested. He is the chief of the *kwatas,* or police, and occupies the same position as he does among us. As insignia of office, these have on their *mpoks,*[4] which they hang from their sides—loops of rope which they use whenever they require to seize prisoners, but this is seldom the case because people hardly ever resist arrest. I am not certain of their number, although there were thirty or so when we saw them together. All, together with their chief, obey the *mfumo-nseba,*[5] who uses them to keep watch over foreigners. Subordinate to the *kakwata* is his delegate, the *katamatwi,* a name which literally signifies "cutter of ears." He is the executioner-in-chief, and on days of *mutentamo,* or audience, the *katamatwi* stands in front of the *kwatas* who are drawn up in close column ten or twelve paces to Kazembe's right. The *kakwata* remains near them, but seated.

[1] The royal enclosure.
[2] Wives' enclosure adjacent to the royal enclosure.
[3] Graves of Kazembes.
[4] Lunda broadswords.
[5] Official in charge of foreign visitors.

In each street there is a *mwine*, or kind of judge, who is responsible for everything that occurs in it, and all small matters involving the street in question are judged by him. But the parties may appeal to the *mwaniasita* to whom the *mwines* are subordinate, and from him also appeal may be made to Kazembe, from whom there is no further appeal; but they would not in any case dare to question his decision. These *mwines* have as their insignia a small hoe stuck into the end of a long cane, with a small iron ring set in such a way in the tenon of the hoe that it tinkles when they lean on it.

In each *mashamo* there is an officer called *mwine-mashamo*, whose duty it is to receive and present the gifts and offerings to the *muzimos*;[6] and, in other respects as well, they are the servants of the *mashamos*.

Kasembe, who is the absolute master of every person and thing, receives the tribute, which he imposes according to his caprice, from the owners of the land. He has no expenditure, fixed or otherwise, save what he distributes as gifts or favors. The *mwata's* will is law; he passes different sentences according to his will and caprice.

There is no kind of legislation known, and the little there is of traditional law relates to the political branch. Everything is decided according to the interest, safety, and convenience of the *mwata*. In fact, the position is such that the man whom yesterday he absolved, today he may condemn to death.

30 / SOCIAL COURTESIES AMONG THE MARAVE

On his way to Lunda, Gamitto passed through the kingdoms of the Marave peoples, to the north of the Zambezi. They were, like the Lunda, strongly influenced by the Luba.[1] Many African peoples have their particular greeting formalities, similar to those described here.

The usual rites of courtesy followed by the Marave are these. People of the same class meeting one another greet without stopping,

From A. C. P. Gamitto, *King Kazembe and the Marave, Cheva, Bisa, Bemba, Lunda and Other Peoples of Southern Africa*. Translated by Ian Cunnison (Lisbon, 1960), Vol. I, p. 107.

[6] Ancestral spirits.
[1] See extract 29.

touching with the palm of one hand the corresponding thigh or buttock; and they do the same on entering a *nyumba*,[2] accompanying this action by bending the knees. But when they wish to speak they sit in silence on the ground, facing one another and holding the left hand open palm upward, navel height; they clap it with their right hand, more quietly each time until in the end it is not heard; then they give five or six claps slowly, and finally two or three loud ones; all this without uttering a word. When the compliment is finished, they begin to speak, and from the beginning they offer each other tobacco which they carry in a little gourd tied to the *musife,* the belt-cord, or by a string round the neck. This tobacco gourd is called *tekue.*

The one offering it hands the *tekue* to the other, who takes it by the bottom with the thumb and middle finger of the same hand; and with the middle finger of the right hand he taps the gourd to shake the tobacco out into his palm, at the same time stopping the gourd with the right hand; then he hands it back. The both of them start taking the snuff in great pinches with thumb and middle finger, accompanying each pinch with a sound like a sneeze, only much louder. And so they go on and use up all the tobacco, and any which might remain in the palm is rubbed on the nose, and the palm is well cleaned. For this reason the Marave always have their upper lips and cheeks soiled with tobacco. It is the fashion.

31 / FUNERAL OF A CHEVA CHIEF

[*The Cheva are a branch of the Marave peoples.*]

From the moment of death all the women of the deceased are guarded with the utmost vigilance and kept in their own *nyumbas,*[1] not in the hut in which the body is lying.

Before the death occurs, it is the *musano,* or first wife, who stays with the sick man along with another or others of his favorites; and these remain there in the same way after his death. Since the death

From A. C. P. Gamitto, *King Kazembe and the Marave, Cheva, Bisa, Bemba, Lunda and Other Peoples of Southern Africa.* Translated by Ian Cunnison (Lisbon, 1960), Vol. I, pp. 145-46.

[2] A house.
[1] Houses.

is kept secret, questions which people ask the dead man are answered by some confidant who speaks in imitation of his voice: this
is to delude the people, who fear that death has taken place. In the
end, once all the relatives, *mambos, fumos,*[2] etc., have gathered, the
death is announced, and from this moment all the wives are shut up
in the same house as the body. When everything is ready for the
burial, the body is carried in the same way as among the Marave,
and all the women follow behind, some with pots, of supurating
matter, others with cloths, etc. If on the way one of the wretched
women has the misfortune to sneeze, she then has to flee, because
it means she is rejected by the dead man's *muzimo.*[3]

When the procession arrives at the graveyard and the grave has
been dug deep enough, the *musano,* or principal wife, goes into it
and sits with her legs out at the place where the corpse's feet will
be. One of the favorite wives sits in the same way at the opposite
end; they face one another with their feet touching. If there are
many wives, they are placed two at the head and two at the foot in
the way stated, and two also at each side with their feet pointing
towards the center. The unfortunate women thus form a platform;
one or more cloths are spread over their legs, upon which they
place the body and the pots, and cover everything with other cloths.
They then seize the remaining wives, and especially the favorites if
there are any of these left, and throw up to six of them into the
grave, first strangling them. They put them on top of the corpse,
and cover the whole with cloths. Then at once they fill in the grave
with soil, and this takes only a moment because the whole crowd
works at it with great haste.

They finish the funeral off by seizing two Negro slaves, who are
still young, strangling them and impaling them from anus to skull
with sharp stakes. These they fasten into the ground, in an upright
position, one slave at the head and the other at the foot of the
grave, facing one another. A small *goma,* or drum, is hung around
the neck of one, and in his right hand, lifted up in the posture of
beating the drum, a drumstick is held; the other they arm with a
bow and arrow, and posture him as if he were in the act of shooting.

The women are buried with the body to accompany the *mambo*

[2] Chiefs.
[3] Spirit.

or *fumo* that he may not be without them, and his spirit may not be left without some state. The two Negroes placed above the grave are destined to put hyenas to flight when they come to dig up the corpse.

32 / THE MONOMOTAPA EMPIRE IN 1517

Duarte Barbosa was in the Portuguese service in India. When he returned to Portugal around 1517 he wrote detailed descriptions of the trading stations of the Indian Ocean. In his descriptions of Sofala, on the east African coast, he included information he had collected about the inland empire of the Monomotapa, which, with its eastern border very close to the coast at Sofala, was the basis of Sofala's trade. The people over whom the Monomotapa ruled were Shonas.

Beyond this country [Sofala] toward the interior lies the great kingdom of Monomotapa, pertaining to the heathen whom the Moors name Kaffirs. They are black men and go naked save that they cover their private parts with cotton cloth from the waist down. Some are clad in skins of wild beasts, and some, the most noble, wear capes of these skins with the tails which trail on the ground, as a token of state and dignity. They leap as they go, and sway their bodies, [and the tails which they wear] fly from one side to the other. They carry swords thrust into wooden scabbards bound with much gold and other metals, worn on the left side, as with us, in cloth girdles which they make for this purpose with four or five knots with hanging tassels to denote men of rank. They also carry assegais in their hands, and other bows and arrows of middle size. The arrows are not so long as those of the English, and not so short as those of the Turks. The iron arrowheads are long and finely pointed. They are warlike men, and some too are great traders. Their women go naked, only covering their private parts with cotton cloths as long as they are unmarried. But when they are married and have borne sons they throw other cloths across their breasts.

Duarte Barbosa. From *The Book of Duarte Barbosa*, edited by M. L. Dames (London: Hakluyt Society, 1918), Vol. I, pp. 8-10.

Fifteen or twenty days' journey inland there is a great town called Zimbabwe,[1] in which there are many houses of wood and of straw. It pertains to the heathen, and the king of Monomotapa often stays there. It is six days' journey thence to Monomotapa. The road thereto goes inland from Sofala towards the Cape of Good Hope. In this town of Monomotapa is the king's most usual abode, in a very large building. And thence the traders carry the inland gold to Sofala and give it unweighed to the Moors for colored cloths and beads, which are greatly esteemed among them; which beads come from Cambaya.[2] As regards Monomotapa these Moors say that the gold comes from a place yet further away towards the Cape of Good Hope, from another kingdom subject to the king of Monomotapa, who is a great lord, with many kings under him. He is lord of an exceeding great country, which runs far inland, and also extends as well to the Cape of Good Hope and Mozambique. Rich presents are daily laid before him, which the other kings and lords send him, each according to his ability. These they carry uncovered on their heads through the town, until they arrive at a very lofty house where the king is always lodged; and he sees them through a window but they see him not, they only hear his voice. Afterward the king sends for the person who has brought him such a present, and soon dismisses him after he has been well entertained. This king always takes with him into the field a captain, whom they call Sono, with a great band of warriors, and five or six thousand women, who also bear arms and fight. With this army he goes about subduing kings who have risen or would rise against their lord.

The king of Monomotapa every year sends men of rank from his kingdom to all the seigniories and places which he holds, to give them new fire, that he may know whether they are obedient to him, in this wise. Each of these men when he arrives at each town has every fire put out, so that not one fire is left in the place. And when all are out, they all come and receive fire from his hand in token of the greatest friendship and obedience. So much so, that the place or town which is not willing to do so is forthwith accused of rebellion. Thereupon the king at once sends his aforesaid captain, who either destroys the seigniory or reduces it to subjection. This cap-

[1] Zimbabwe was the name always given to the capitals of these Shona states.
[2] Port of Cambay in Gujarat, India.

tain, with all his warriors, wheresoever he wishes to stay, is fed at the cost of the town. Their provisions are millet, rice, and flesh. They also make use of gingelly oil.

33 / THE KINGDOM OF THE KITEVE IN THE LATE SIXTEENTH CENTURY

In July 1590, John dos Santos, a Dominican priest, went six hundred miles up the Zambeze to Tete, where he remained until May 1591. As a result of this and other African travels, he published Ethiopia Oriental *at Evora in 1609. Samuel Purchas[1] translated a brief version of it, from which the following passages are taken. The people of the kingdom of the Kiteve, like those of the Monomotapa's empire, were Shonas.*

Of Kiteve, King of That Country, with the Strange Customs Observed in Those Parts, in Court, City, and Country

The king of these parts is of curled hair, a gentile, which worships nothing, nor hath any knowledge of God; yea, rather he carries himself as God of his countries, and so is holden and reverenced of his vassals. He is called Kiteve, a title royal and no proper name, which they exchange for this so soon as they become kings. The Kiteve hath more than one hundred women all within doors, amongst which one or two are his queens, the rest as concubines. Many of them are his own aunts, cousins, sisters, and daughters, which he no less useth, saying that his sons by them are true heirs of the kingdom without mixture of other blood. When the Kiteve dieth, his queens must die with him to do him service in the other world; who accordingly at the instant of his death take a poison (which they call *lucasse*) and die therewith. The successor succeedeth as well to the women as the state. None else but the king may, upon pain of death, marry his sister or daughter. This successor is commonly one of the eldest sons of the deceased king, and of his great women or queens; and if the eldest be not sufficient, then the next, or if none of them be fit, his brother of whole blood. The king commonly, while he liveth, maketh the choice, and trains

John dos Santos, "Eastern Ethiopia." From *Hakluytus Posthumus or Purchas His Pilgrimes* (Glasgow, 1905), Vol. IX, pp. 203-214.

[1] See introduction to extract 28.

up him to affairs of state, to whom he destines the succession. Whiles I lived there . . . the king had above thirty sons, and yet showed more respect to his brother, a wise man, than to any of them, all honoring him as apparent heir.

The same day the king dies, he is carried to a hill where all the kings are interred. And early the next morning, he whom the king had named his successor goeth to the king's house where the king's women abide in expectation, and by their consent he enters the house, and seats himself with the principal of them in a public hall, where the king was wont to sit to hear causes, in a place drawn with curtains or covered with a cloth, that none may see the king nor the women with him. And thence he sends his officers, which go through the city and proclaim festivals to the new king, who is now quietly possessed of the king's house, with the women of the king deceased, and that all should go and acknowledge him for the king: which is done by all the great men then in court, and the nobles of the city, who go to the palace now solemnly guarded, and enter into the hall by licence of the officers, where the new king abides with his women; entering some, and some creeping on the ground till they come to the middle of the hall, and thence speak to the new king, giving him due obeisance, without seeing him or his women. The king makes answer from within, and accepts their service: and after that draws the curtains, and shows himself to them; whereat all of them clap their hands, and then turn behind the curtains, and go forth creeping on the ground as they came in. And when they are gone, others enter and do in like sort. In this ceremony the greatest part of the day is spent with feasting, music, and dancing through the city. The next day the king sends his officers through the kingdom to declare this his succession, and that all should come to the court to see him break the bow. Sometimes there are many competitors, and then he succeeds whom the women admit into the king's house. For none may enter by law without their leave, nor can be king without peaceable entrance—forceable entry forfeiting his right and title. By bribes, therefore, and other ways, they seek to make the women on their side.

Near the kingdom of Kiteve is another of laws and customs like thereto, where the Sedanda reigns: both of which were sometimes but one kingdom. Whiles I was in Sofala, the Sedanda being incurably sick of a leprosy, declared his successor, and poisoned himself: which also is the custom there, if any king have any deformity in his person. The named successor sought admittance of the women. But they, much distasting him, had secretly sent by night for another prince whom they better liked, as more valiant and better beloved; whom they admitted, and assembled themselves with him in the public hall, and caused proclamation to be made to the people of his succession. The other, whom they had rejected, fled for fear of his life, and, being mighty, assembled a great power, and by force entered the king's house. But this was strange to all, who therefore forsook him, and stuck to him whom the women had chosen. Whereupon the other fled and no more lifted up his head.

Before the new king begins to govern, he sends for all the chiefs in the kingdom, to come to the court and see him break the king's bow, which is all one with taking possession of the kingdom. In those courts is a custom then also to kill some of those lords or great men, saying they are necessary for the service of the deceased king; whereupon they kill those of whom they stand in fear or doubt, or whom they hate, in stead of whom they make and erect new lords. This custom causeth such as fear themselves to flee the land. Anciently the kings were wont to drink poison in any grievous disasters, as in a contagious disease, or natural impotency, lameness, the loss of their fore-teeth, or other deformity; saying that kings ought to have no defect. Which if it happened, it was honor for him to die, and go to better himself in that better life, in which he should be wholly perfect. But the Kiteve which reigned while I was there, would not follow his predecessors herein; but having lost one of his fore-teeth, sent to proclaim through his kingdom that one of his teeth were fallen out, and (that they might not be ignorant when they saw him want it) that if his predecessors were such fools, for such causes to kill themselves, he would not do so, but await his natural death, holding his life necessary to conserve his estate against his enemies, which example he would commend to posterity.

If the Kaffirs have a suit, and seek to speak with the king, they creep to the place where he is, having prostrated themselves at the entrance, and look not on him all the while they speak, but lying on one side clap their hands all the time (a rite of obsequiousness in those parts), and then, having finished, they creep out of the doors as they came in. For no Kaffir may enter on foot to speak to the king, nor eye him in speaking, except the familiars and particular friends of the king. . . .

Every September the Kiteve, at the change of the moon, goeth from Zimbabwe[1] his city to a high hill to perform obits or obsequies to his predecessors there buried, with great troops both of the city and other parts of the kingdoms called up therefore. As soon as they are ascended, they eat and drink their *pombe*,[2] the king beginning, till they be all drunk; continuing their eating and drinking eight days, one of which they call Pemberar of a kind of tilting exercise then used. In this feast the king and his nobles clothe themselves in their best silks and cotton clothes, which they have with many thrums, like carpet fringes, wrought therein, hanging down on the eyes and face as a horse's fore-top. They tie about the head a large ribbon, and divided into two parts, they run one against another on foot with bows and arrows in their hands, which they shoot upwards that none be hurt; and thus make a thousand careers and feats till they be tired and cannot stir. And they which hold out longest are accounted the valiantest properest men, and are therefore rewarded with the prize propounded. . . .

After this eight days' festival, they spend two days or three in mourning. And then the devil enters into one of the company, saying he is the soul of the deceased king, father of the present, to whom those obsequies are performed; and that he comes to speak to his son. The Kaffir thus possessed falls down on the ground in an ill plight and is distracted, the devil speaking by his mouth all the strange tongues of all the Kaffir nations about them, many of which some of the men present understand. After this, he begins to behave himself and to speak like the king pretended, by which signs the Kaffirs acknowledge the coming of the deceased king's soul. The king is now made acquainted herewith, and comes with his grands to the place where the demoniac is, and do him great reverence. Then all the rest go aside, and the king remains with him alone, speaking friendly as with his father departed, and inquireth if he be to make wars, whether he shall overcome his enemies, touching dearth, or troubles in his kingdom, and whatever else he desireth to know. And the devil answereth his questions, and adviseth him what to do.

[1] The capital.
[2] Beer.

The Kiteve has two or three hundred men for his guard, which are his officers and executioners, called *inficia,* and go crying, "Inhama, inhama," that is "Flesh, flesh." He hath another sort called *marombes,* jesters, which have their songs and prose in praise of the king, whom they call, Lord of the Sun and Moon, King of the Land and Rivers, Conqueror of his Enemies, in everything great, great thief, great witch, great lion; and all other names of greatness which they can invent, whether they signify good or bad, they attribute to them. When the king goeth out of doors, these *marombes* go round about him with great cries of this argument. He hath others which are musicians in his hall, and at the court gates, with divers instruments resounding his praises. Their best musical instrument is called *ambira,* much like to our organs. . . .

They use three kinds of oath in judgement most terrible, in accusations wanting just evidence. The first is called *Lucasse,* which is a vessel full of poison, which they give the suspected, with words importing his destruction and present death if he be guilty, his escape if innocent. The terror whereof makes the conscious confess the crime. But the innocent drink it confidently without harm, and thereby are acquitted of the crime. And the plaintiff is condemned to him whom he falsely had accused; his wife, children, and goods being forfeited, one moiety to the king, and the other to the defendant.

The second oath they call *xoqua,* which is made by iron heated red hot in the fire, causing the accused to lick it being so hot with his tongue, saying, that the fire shall not hurt him if he be innocent; otherwise it shall burn his tongue and mouth. . . .

The third oath they call Calano, which is a vessel of water made bitter with certain herbs which they put into it, whereof they give the accused to drink, saying that if he be innocent he shall drink it all off at one gulp without any stay, and cast it all up again at once without any harm. If guilty he shall not be able to get down one drop without gargling and choking.

The Kiteve makes some royal huntings, with three or four thousand men, in the deserts near the city: encircling all the beasts in that compass, tigers, lions, ounces, elephants, buffalos, deer, wild swine, and the rest, driving them together, and then setting on their dogs, with cries, arrows, and assegais, pursue and kill what they can. Then may they kill the lion, which at other times by the Ki-teve's prohibition is a deadly offence, because he is entitled Great Lion. After this they eat in the same place with great jollity; but the most they carry home, and hang it for the king and for themselves.

Their houses are round, of unhewn timber covered with straw, like a thatched country house, which they remove at pleasure.

The Kaffirs buy of the parents their wives, for kine, clothes, or otherwise, according to their ability. And therefore they that have many daughters are rich. If any mislike his wife, he may return her to him that sold her, but with loss of the price paid; and the parent may sell her again to another husband. The wife has no liberty to forsake her husband. The ceremonies of marriage are dances and feastings of the neighbors; every invited guest bringing his present of meal, maize, inhames, fitches, or other victuals for that day's expenses. He which is able may have two wives, but few are able to maintain them, except the great men which have many, but one is principal, the rest as handmaids. Some of them live like wild beasts, and when they are near time of travail, they go to the wilderness or untilled places, and there go up and down receiving the savor of that wild place, which causeth to them quicker delivery. They, after their delivery, wash themselves and their children in a lake or river, and then return to their houses with them in their arms without swaddling them.

34 / THE JOURNEY OF THE CASTAWAYS OF THE ST. JOHN THE BAPTIST FROM THE KEISKAMA RIVER TO SOFALA, 1622-23

While on a voyage between Goa and Lisbon in July 1622, the Portuguese carrack St. John the Baptist, *commanded by Captain Peter de Morais Sarmento, encountered two Dutch East Indiamen in the Indian Ocean, south of latitude 35° south. The great sea fight that ensued lasted for nineteen days, by which time the ships were in latitude 42° south. The* St. John the Baptist *was hopelessly crippled. Leaking, dismasted, rudderless, and at the mercy of the icy*

Francis Vaz d'Almada. From *The Tragic History of the Sea, 1589-1622,* by C. R. Boxer (Cambridge: Hakluyt Society Publication, Series II, number cxii, 1959), pp. 197-261. Reprinted by permission of Cambridge University Press.

storms of the roaring forties, she nonetheless eventually made a landfall on September 29th, on a wild and rocky stretch of the south African coast. The place is thought to have been near the Keiskama river, a little to the south of East London. From there the survivors made a hazardous overland journey to Sofala; many died on the way. Their story, first published in Lisbon in 1625, is told by Francis Vaz d'Almada, a soldier returning from service in India. Although hastily compiled and sometimes vague, it provides an authentic eye-witness account of the longest journey ever made by Portuguese castaways in southeast Africa. The passages given here are those which describe the native peoples encountered by the party. Contact with natives was slight, but the narrative has historical importance, for it shows how far the southward movement of Bantu-speaking peoples had reached by the first quarter of the seventeenth century.

. . . The necessary provisions and weapons were landed, though with great difficulty, for it was a wild coast, so that every time the boat approached the shore to disembark something, it was necessary to anchor with a grapnel by the stern and wade ashore holding on to the line in order to keep head-on to waves; so much so, that once when they did not anchor by the stern, eighteen persons were drowned in landing one boatload. This was the reason why we did not afterward try to build a boat, for this coast is so stormy that we feared that after it was made we would not be able to launch it.

On the 3rd October, while we were completing the landing of the things needed for the overland journey and building shacks to shelter us from the excessive cold of that region during the time we remained there, the men who kept watch raised the alarm that Negroes[1] were approaching. We took up arms, and, as they drew near to us, they handed the assegais which they carried to their children until they were very close to us, when they squatted down on their haunches, clapping their hands and whistling softly, in such a way that they all kept in tune together, and many women who were with them began to dance. These Negroes are whiter than mulattoes; they are stoutly built men, and disfigure themselves with daubs of ocher, charcoal, and ashes, with which they generally paint their faces, though they are really quite good looking.

[1] They were evidently Hottentots.

On this first meeting they brought as a present a very fine large ox and a leather bag of milk, which the king gave to Roderick Affonso de Mello, who was acting as captain at the time, Peter de Morais being still aboard the ship. The courtesy which this king did to the aforesaid captain was to stroke his beard many times. After we had given some pieces of iron hoops and *bertangils*[2] as a return present to the king, he went to the ox and ordered it to be cut open alive at the navel, and he with most of those who were with him plunged their hands into the entrails of the ox while it was still alive and bellowing, smearing themselves with that filth. We realized that they performed all these ceremonies as a sign of good faith and friendship. They then cut up the ox into quarters and gave it to us, keeping for themselves the hide and entrails, which they placed on embers and devoured on the spot.

During the month and six days that we remained in that place we could never understand a word these people said, for their speech is not like that of mankind, and when they want to say anything they make clicks with the mouth,[3] one at the beginning, another in the middle, and another at the end; so that it may be deduced from these people that the earth is not all one, nor all mankind alike. . . .

During this time we bartered for cows, which we ate, though they were not as many as we needed. We kept those which seemed fit for work in a stockade, accustoming them to carry pack-saddles, which were very well made out of carpets, for there were not wanting workmen in the camp who knew how to make them. . . .

On the 6th November we set out from that land in Latitude 30° south in a column of march, two hundred and seventy-nine persons divided into four bodies. . . .

This day was a very rainy one, and, as things were not yet very well arranged, we marched for a league and then pitched camp on the bank of a fresh-water river, where we passed a bad night on account of the incessant rain. This land is intersected with rivers of very good water, and firewood is available, but there is a lack of fruit and provisions, though it seems as if the soil would yield abundant crops of anything sown in it. The inhabitants thereof

[2] Cotton piece goods from India.
[3] The clicks are typical of Hottentot speech.

live solely on shellfish, some roots which look like truffles, and the produce of the chase. They have no knowledge of any seed planting, or of any other kind of provisions. Even so, they are vigorous and courageous, capable of performing feats of strength and agility, for they will pursue a bull and hold it fast, though these animals are of the most monstrous size imaginable.

The next day, the 7th November, we continued our journey, keeping always close to the shore. When we had gone about three leagues we made our camp in the afternoon on the bank of a river, pitching our tents in a circle, within which we put the cows at night, posting sentinels and making the rounds with great care and vigilance. But this did not suffice to prevent the Kaffirs from stealing all the cattle, though they did not get away scot-free. For as these Kaffirs are great hunters, they always have their hunting dogs with them, and these cows are reared with the dogs who guard them from the lions and tigers on this coast; and at their approach, these dogs rouse the cattle by barking, and thus they are always together and mingle with each other, and even though they are brute beasts they know and make much of each other. And as the cows were leaving the land where they had been reared, they lowed continually, as if in longing; and during the third watch the Kaffirs[4] came and let loose the dogs inside with low whistling and shouts, and the cows when they heard them jumped through the tents and fled with the dogs behind them. We followed, fighting with the Kaffirs, and we killed the son of their king and many of his company, and they wounded three of our men. This day was a very sad one for us, for they carried off our cows which were laden with all our provisions, and which could have been used themselves for the same purpose.

We had with us a Kaffir who turned up at the place where we landed, a native of the island of Angoxa,[5] who was the only one that our Kaffir slaves could understand. He was a prisoner because he had promised to come and guide us but later did not wish to do so, and thus we were obliged to take him along as captive. This man told us that within twenty days as the Kaffirs travel, which would be about two months at our rate, we would reach a region

[4] Evidently the same group of Hottentots as those encountered on October 3rd.
[5] Angoche—a chain of islands in the Mozambique channel.

where there were cows, but it was all a wilderness as far as that; as we afterward found by experience, it extended much farther than he said.

We continued our journey until about the 15th of December, when we reached a river where we arrived half-dead with hunger. . . .

Here I was involved in an incident which I have sufficient confidence in your worship[6] to tell you about, and also because it was well known to all. While we were still on the hillside, before we came down to the river, the captain bade me go forward about a league with fifteen arquebusiers to see if we could discover a village, for we had now reached the region where the Kaffir had told us that we would find cows. Having advanced about half a league along the river that was winding through a plain, I saw a hamlet of fifteen straw huts, and in order not to alarm the Kaffirs I ordered six men to advance and see if there was any kind of food that they would sell us. But they declined to obey, on the plea that there seemed to be many people in the village and that we would be too far off to help them if they got into difficulties. This vexed me, and after arguing angrily with them I chose the four best arquebusiers present, who were John Ribeiro, Cyprian Dias, Francis Luis, and the ship's steward, with whom I descended the hill and crossed a valley which lay between us and the Negroes' kraal, in which there was a river then at high tide, and we forded it with the water to our chests.

Having reached the entrance of their enclosure, we asked them to sell us something to eat, speaking to them by signs, and putting our hands to our mouths; for by carelessness or forgetfulness we had not brought an interpreter with us to explain what we wanted, nor had we asked the captain for one, although these Kaffirs could understand the Negro slaves we had brought from India.[7] They were amazed at seeing us white and clothed, and the women and children made a great hullabaloo, calling to the people of another kraal which was in the bush. [We retired] and their husbands who were with them followed us closely, throwing fire-hardened sticks at us. Seeing the harm which they might do us, I ordered John

6 The treatise was addressed to the Secretary of the Portuguese Council of the Exchequer.

7 This suggests that they were Bantu-speaking people.

Ribeiro to fire at them with an arquebus, which he immediately did, but it did not go off, and the Kaffirs grew more enraged, thinking that the making of the flame was witchcraft. Seeing the danger we were in, I took careful aim with my matchlock and killed three with a single shot, for I always fired with one [ordinary] bullet and three shaped like dice. These deaths caused great consternation among them, and the survivors broke off their pursuit of us. . . .

On returning to where the captain was, I made him a fine present of squabs, with which he was very pleased, and when he was well satisfied with the sight of something so very desirable and estimable in a time of such real hunger, we told him what had happened to us. He was much upset at this, and I did not doubt that if anything untoward had happened as a result of this incident I would have paid dearly for it, for every transgression was most rigorously punished. Earlier this same day, as the captain was going down to the river he saw a Kaffir, who on being interrogated said that there were some cows and garden plots further on. Then the captain asked Roderick Affonso de Mello to go with twenty men and see what was to be found. The Negro went with him, but afterward told them to return, as it was getting late, promising to come the next day and guide them to the place he had spoken of. Roderick Affonso at once turned back, and, passing by the village where we had killed the three Negroes, he found them still unburied, and the Negroes pointed them out with great fear and trembling, to the amazement of Roderick Affonso, for he did not know what had happened. They told him that the dead were to blame, because they had begun the war, and so they had reported to their king; and they gave him some of the produce from their garden plot, consisting of calabashes and green watermelons. Roderick Affonso gave them two little pieces of copper, which is the best article for barter in these parts, and went on his way back.

The next day the same Kaffir came again, and Roderick Affonso set off with him, and they traveled for a day and a night. Journeying farther on, he met in a valley the son of the king of whom the Kaffir had spoken, accompanied by a hundred Kaffir warriors all well armed with iron assegais. . . .

Journeying on a few days, we came to a river where there was a village of fisher-folk upon a height on the side in the direction of the Cape [of Good Hope], and we pitched our camp on the other bank. They brought us for sale a small quantity of dough made from some seeds smaller than mustard which come from a herb that sticks to one's clothes. It tasted very good to those who were able to get any of it.

We slept that night in a valley where the long grass stood higher than a lance. Next day we rose early in the morning and marched up a hillside through some pleasant country. On meeting some Negroes we asked them about the villages, and they replied that if we walked fast we would reach them when the sun was in the meridian. Being eager and in want, though weak, we kept on climbing, and in the afternoon we reached the top of a range from which we had the most beautiful view that our eyes could desire, for many valleys lay before us, intersected by rivers and smaller hills, in which were an infinite number of villages with herds of cattle and garden plots. At this sight we descended the hillside very joyfully, and the Kaffirs came out to meet us on our way, bringing jars of milk and cows for sale.

Next day we climbed to the top of that range, which was very high, in quest of a village where dwelt the king of that whole district. We reached it in the afternoon, and it was the largest we had yet seen. The king, who was blind, came to visit the captain, and brought him a present of a little millet in a calabash. Though old, he was a healthy looking man. It is worthy of note that, though they are savages without any knowledge of the truth, they have such a serious mien and are so respected by their subjects, that I cannot exaggerate it. They rule and punish them in such a way that they keep them quiet and obedient. They have their laws, and they punish adulterers gallantly in the following manner: if a woman is guilty of adultery toward her husband, and he can prove it by witnesses, she is ordered to be put to death, together with the adulterer if they can catch him, whose wives the aggrieved husband then marries.

When anyone wishes to marry, the king makes the match, so that no marriage can take place unless he names the bride. It is their custom when their sons are ten years old to turn them into the bush, where they clothe themselves from the waist downward with the leaves of a tree like the palm, and rub themselves with ashes till they look as if they were whitewashed. They all keep together in a body, but they do not come to the village, their mothers taking food to them in the bush. These boys have the duty of dancing at weddings and feasts which it is customary to hold, and they are paid with cows, calves, and goats where there are any. When anyone of them has got together in this way some three or four head of cattle, and has reached the age of over eighteen years, his father or mother goes to their king and tells him that they have a son of fitting age who by his own exertions has gained so many head of cattle, and the said father or mother is willing to help him by giving him something further, and they request the king to give him a wife. The king then replies: "Go to such a place, and tell so-and-so to bring his daughter here." When they come, he arranges about the dowry which the husband is obliged to pay his father-in-law, and the king's palms are always greased in making these contracts. This is the custom[8] as far as Inhaca Manganheira, which is the river of Lourenco Marques.

All these Kaffirs wear cloaks of very well-dressed skins, which hang below their hips. The skins are those of small animals with beautiful fur, and these furs vary according to the quality of the Kaffir who wears them, and they are very punctilious about this. They wear nothing but these capes and a politer skin which covers their privy parts. I saw a grave Kaffir with a cloak of sable skins, and when I asked him where these animals were to be found, he said that there were so many of them farther inland, that nearly everyone wore them.

I also found upon the ground two assegais and a little piece of wood of the thickness of a finger and about two and a half spans long, covered from the middle upward with a monkey's tail. It is customary to carry a stick of this kind throughout almost the whole of Kaffraria as far as the river of Lourenco Marques, and they never converse without it, for they emphasize all their talk by gesticulating with this stick in their hand, and they call it their mouth, making gestures and grimaces.

[8] He is evidently describing customs associated with Bantu-speaking people.

On the second day of February, Candlemas Day, after marching all the morning we dined in a beautiful wood, through which flowed a stream of water. . . .

Next day we reached the kraals of the longed-for plenty, where they at once brought for sale many goats, cows, cakes as big as Flemish cheeses, and so much millet that afterward we could not carry it all. Here the captain ordered eighteen goats and a cow to be killed, and each one of us received six pounds at his share. They also brought so many hens that each person had one, and the food was so plentiful that we would all have died if we had not been attacked by diarrhea.

On the following day the *manamuze*[9] of these places came to visit us, and he brought a very large bull as a present. The captain ordered me to kill it with my matchlock, so that they might hear it, for the chief had many men with him, and also they might see what weapons we possessed. When they saw the bull fall dead, though I fired at it from a great distance, the king took to flight, so that we had to send and tell him that this was done to celebrate his arrival to see us, and that he should return, for otherwise the captain would have to go and fetch him. Hearing these arguments he came back, but in such a state that from black he had turned white. The captain hung round his neck the lock of a gilt writing box, and I gave him the handle of a cauldron. He valued these things highly, and withdrew with friendly words and a show of gratitude. . . .

We marched along on the tops of the hills, on the slopes of which there were so many and such fine looking kraals that it was admirable to see the great quantity of cattle which came out of them. They brought us along the wayside a lot of milk for sale, but it was all sour, for the Kaffirs do not drink it otherwise.

At midday we pitched our camp by a fresh river in a valley, and thither came many Kaffirs, all bringing something for sale. We did the usual barter trade on the other side of the river apart from the tents, with men keeping guard. We did this here with greater precaution because more Kaffirs came than ever we had seen before, and their numbers were so great that many of them climbed up the trees merely to see us, especially on the top of three trees at the feet of which the bartering was carried on, because they

[9] Chief or king.

sheltered us from the sun, so that I do not know how they did not break beneath so great a weight. Truly a fine picture could have been painted of that place and the concourse of people. We remained there until the afternoon, and afterward we bought fifteen cows and many cakes, so that we were all more heavily laden.

We remained here for two days in which the carpenter, Vincent Esteves, made a raft like a boat, which was rowed with four oars. During this time the very Kaffirs who had attacked us came to sell us hens, cakes, and *pombe*,[10] which is a wine that they make from millet. We dissimulated, pretending not to know them, and bought from them what we needed. Other Kaffirs also came from the other side of the river to sell us the same things, crossing the river on pieces of wood, with a kind of pitchfork high above the water, from which their merchandise was suspended. These people asked us why we had killed so many of the others, and when we told them what had happened to us, they told us to cross over to the other side, as they were bad people on this. They said they would show us where we could cross the river three days later, for now the water was high and it would be lower then. . . .

Thence we marched onward for two days, keeping within two leagues of the shore, and at the end of that time we came to a river which looked like a lagoon, and debouched on to the beach. Here we saw an elephant with a young one, and as the rear guard was coming along later they saw many elephants, which took no notice of us, nor in all this journey did they do us any harm at all. Having crossed this river at the mouth, with the water up to our necks, we went on along the shore until we came to another river with many large rocks at the mouth, and we could not cross it because the water was too deep. Climbing up a steep hill, we saw some Kaffirs who said they would show us the ford, and for a few little pieces of copper they carried over the children and many persons who were sick. This people thenceforward are of a better type, and we called them the Naunetas, because when they met us they said "Naunetas," which in their language means "you are welcome," and to this greeting the reply is "Alaba," which means "and you also." Here they sold us a great quantity of fish, and they

[10] The Bantu word for beer.

helped us to carry the loads which our Negroes bore, singing and clapping their hands.

Thence we went and slept on the edge of the beach, where the king of the country, whom they call Manamuze, came to see us. He was a youth, and came in a very dignified fashion with three brass collars round his neck, brass being valued above all else in those parts. On seeing him coming, the captain took him a little silver bell, which was incomparably more valuable to the king, and wearing his scarlet cloak he approached the spot where the king was waiting. They greeted each other, the Kaffir losing nothing of his high bearing; but when the captain saw his attitude, he began to move his body so that the bell rang, at which they were all astonished, and the king could contain himself no longer. Taking the bell in his hand, he looked inside to see what it was that made it ring, and moving it and ringing it, he laughed loudly the while, never taking his eyes off it all the time that he was there.

It is a remarkable thing how these brutes are respected in their way; and in their different generations and families they are so united that their sons never lose the places and kraals which are left them by their fathers. The eldest son inherits everything, the others calling him father and respecting him as such. Thieves are cruelly punished (though they are all thieves), and they have a jocund mode of justice which is as follows. If a Kaffir steals a kid or something trifling from another, the owner of the kid and his relatives can pass on the culprit what sentence they choose, which is usually that he be buried alive. Here they sold us a very large fat ox, and these they call *zembe*.

Next day we journeyed over some barren plains, and there came to meet us a Kaffir with a round brass ornament hung round his neck, which covered all his breast, and he bade us go with him and he would lead us to a place where there were plenty of provisions. He led us along in a river with the water up to our knees, and it was shaded by trees so high and thick that during the two hours we were wading in it we did not see the sun. Having finished with this river, we traveled all that day without stopping, because we had no millet. We reached the kraal in the evening, and seeking to provide ourselves we found only one kind of food, which is the same as that which is given to canaries in Lisbon, and there called *alpiste,* and by the Kaffirs *amechueira.* These people had lured us out of our way simply in order to see us, and they showed great surprise at the sight of us. They asked us the reason why we came through strange lands with our women and children, and when our Kaffirs told them, they twisted their fingers as if invoking curses upon whoever had caused our shipwreck.

Thence we traveled over a flat country inhabited by very poor people who nevertheless received us hospitably. After two days we reached a kraal near the shore, in which we found some fish, and the people showed themselves more compassionate than any we had yet met. For the women and children went down to the beach and threw many stones into the sea, uttering certain words which seemed like curses; and then turning their backs upon it they lifted up the skins which covered their backsides and exhibited their arses to the ocean. This is the worst form of insult which they have, and they did this because they had been told that the sea was the cause of our suffering so many hardships and of our wandering for five months through strange lands. This last was what surprised them most, as they usually never travel ten leagues from the place where they were born, and they look upon that as a far journey.

At this . . . rivulet a child was left behind, the son of Louis da Fonseca and Beatrice Alvarez. He was very emaciated, and had often stayed behind at some of the previous kraals, but the Kaffirs had always brought him along to us the next day, and we thought that the same thing would happen this time.

We marched for another four days along the shore, at the end of which time a Kaffir came to meet us, accompanied by six others. He looked very much a gentleman, and was well adorned with a chain going many times round his neck, a fine piece of cloth round his waist, and both hands full of assegais, for this is the way in which their most important persons deck themselves out. And nothing in these people whom we met, from the remotest tribes in the place where we landed, surprised me more than what I shall now relate. They had so little knowledge of us that they thought we were creatures born in the sea, and they asked us by signs to show our navels, which two sailors immediately did. They then asked us to breathe in and out, and when they saw us do this they nodded their heads, as if to say, "These are human beings like us." All these Kaffirs as far as Sofala are circumcised, and I do not know who went thither and taught them this rite.

This above-mentioned Kaffir was the son of Inhaca Sangane, the legitimate king and lord of the island in the river of Lourenço Marques, whom the Inhaca Manganheira had dispossessed. He resided on the mainland with his followers, awaiting the death of this tyrant, who was very old, to return to his former possession, as I shall relate hereafter. He led us about a league into the interior to his kraals, where they sold us some goats. We asked him to lead us to his father, but he postponed this for a day, hoping that we would buy something more in his territory. Being eager to reach our destination, we would not remain there long, and when we set out again, he ordered the way to be shown us, realizing that nothing would induce us to stay longer. On this line of march we saw a large straw house, and before we reached it we could discern many figures without faces, fashioned like dogs, crocodiles, and men, all made of straw. On asking what they were, I was told that was the house of a Kaffir who gave rain when their garden plots needed it. Witchcraft is their only form of government.

We ate our dinner in the shade of some trees, where they brought us a quantity of honey in the comb for sale. Here a Kaffir who spoke Portuguese came to meet us, bringing a message from the Inhaca Sangane, father of the Kaffir we had met before. The sight of this Kaffir was as joyful news to us, for we were reassured by him, and believed that what they had told us previously was true. He delivered his message, which was that the Inhaca bade us go to where he was, where nothing would be wanting for us, and he would give us a boat in which to cross to the other side of the river, and he would do all we wished. The captain, not trusting to all this, sent a Portuguese to him carrying a present of some articles of copper. This man went and spoke with the Inhaca and many other Kaffirs there, after which he returned, bringing the captain a bunch of bananas, at which we were delighted for they are good Indian fruit. This emissary said that the king seemed to be a good man, and that he had no forces with which he could harm us, and that he was waiting for us, and that his followers said that many Portuguese came there every year. In order to hasten our coming, he sent us a sailor from Mozambique, who had remained there from one of the ships which had visited the bay in past years.

Upon this we set out, and having marched for about a league along the edge of a marsh, we reached the place where the king resided, which was on a height between two small hills. As it was now night, he did not speak to us, but sent his men to show us a place adjoining his kraals where we could pitch our tents. Next day the captain went to see him, and hung a gold chain with the insignia of the Order of Christ[11] round his neck, and gave him two *sarrasas,* a kind of cotton cloth worn by Indian women which is highly valued. He received this with great dignity, and, speaking but a few words, told the captain not to worry for he would leave his lands well content, since he had no greater desire than to be a friend of the Portuguese. Thereupon the captain withdrew. This Negro is a great personage, and was always loyal to the Portuguese.

The next day he came to see us, and ordered goats, sheep, many hens, and *amechueira* to be brought us. But as he delayed showing us a boat which he said he had, we went straight to the beach, and after marching along it for two days we reached the river of Lourenço Marques,[12] which we so greatly desired, on the 6th April 1623. We did not recognize it until we actually reached it, for the above-mentioned island lies very close to the mainland on the side of the Cape of Good Hope, and thus everything looked like a part of the mainland to us as we marched along.

When we had traversed the shore for about a quarter of a league, we pitched our tents and fired a salute of three or four salvoes of matchlocks. As it was then night we lit our fires, and all with Father Diogo dos Anjos, a Capuchin friar, and Father Bento gave thanks to God for having brought us to a place where we were known and whither ships came from Mozambique. Next day we saw two dugout canoes with Negroes who spoke Portuguese very well, whereat we were still more pleased, for hitherto we had not seen a canoe or a boat of any sort. The captain sent to visit the king of the island, who was the Inhaca Manganheira aforesaid, asking him to let us know whether he had provisions upon which we could subsist for the month which we might have to remain there until a vessel could be got ready to take us over to the other

---

[11] The leading Portuguese military order of knighthood.
[12] Delagoa Bay.

side, so that we could reach it in good time to find the ship from Mozambique. The Inhaca replied that we should go to him and he would provide us with everything, sending us three small vessels in which to cross over to the island, which we immediately did.

When all our people had landed on the island, we marched in our usual order to the kraal where the king was. It was composed of large houses with palisaded courtyards, so that they looked like the dwelling place of a warrior. He was seated on a mat, covered with a cinnamon colored serge cape, which seemed to be of English manufacture, and with a hat on his head. Seeing the captain, he arose, but without moving forward, and gave him a hearty embrace. The captain took off the cape which the Inhaca wore, leaving him naked, and covered him with another one of black *capichuela*,[13] and hung round his neck a silver chain with a whistle, which had belonged to the boatswain Manuel Alvares, a thing which he esteemed highly. This Negro looked very old and fat, whereas throughout the whole of Kaffraria I never saw a Kaffir who was round-shouldered or fat, but on the contrary they were all up-standing and lean. He bade us pitch our tents near the kraals, and next day they brought us for sale quantities of fish, hens, and *amechueira,* and a few sheep.

[*The Inhaca Manganheira offered the party hospitality on an island where they could await the arrival of Portuguese ships. But de Morais decided to cross the bay and continue northward, in spite of warnings of the hostile nature of the Mocrangos and others, into whose country they would be proceeding.*]

And now we were entering the country of the robbers, we tried to march on as fast as we could. And so we did fighting continually with them, which we did with great difficulty, being sick and weak, for provisions were scarce and the Kaffirs would not sell us any.

We journeyed thus until we came to the river of Gold,[14] which is very deep and wide, and flows with such fury that more than eight leagues before we reached it we found huge trees torn up by the roots in such quantities that they covered the shore, so that

---

[13] Thought to mean silk.
[14] The Limpopo.

very often we could not pass over them, and as we soon realized we must be approaching some great river. The lord of all this region is a very old Negro whom they call Nyapure.[15] We were greatly distressed at the sight of this river, for we thought it would be impossible to cross it. But before long we saw two dugout canoes coming downstream, at the sight of which our fears diminished. Calling them over toward us, I sent to ask if they would carry us across, to which they replied "yes," and said that they would come next day with more canoes in order to do so. I ordered a piece of *bertangil* [16] to be given them for their favorable answer, and they went away.

As we were waiting for them next morning, the men who were on guard saw advancing on our side of the river over two hundred Kaffirs very well armed with assegais and arrows, and they were the first we had seen with these arms. I at once ranged everyone in order, and fired off several guns. They came to us in a body, with their king in the middle. He was bravely dressed in the Portuguese fashion, with a doublet of *tafecira* inside out, a pair of baggy trousers back to front, and a hat upon his head. He came dressed like this to show that he had dealing with us, and that we might trust him, but his design was immediately perceived.

[*The party crossed the Limpopo, but were then attacked and suffered greatly.*]

On the eve of Pentecost, as we were marching by night, we saw many fires along the shore, from which we concealed ourselves, keeping very close to the sea; and we passed by them very quietly without being seen, pressing forward as quickly as we could until the third watch, when we took cover in the bush. We remained there keeping strict watch until it was night and the tide was half out, when we marched on in orderly fashion until the middle of the second watch, when we saw in front of us many fires which barred our way from the edge of the sea to the bush, so that we could not escape from them.

As we approached, the Mocaranga Muquulo, who was king of all that region, sent to tell us that we must not pass through his

[15] Still the native name for the country round the Limpopo mouth.
[16] Cotton piece goods from India.

country at night, as it was not customary, and that he did not want to fight with us. I [17] sent a reply that the Portuguese required no man's permission to go wherever they wanted. He then sent to tell me to beware of what I did and not to cause a war, for all the Portuguese who passed that way made him a present as they did in other parts. . . .

Thus we journeyed on through the lands of the Zavala, a shaikh or ruler who was our friend, until we met an old Kaffir, the subject of a king named Aquetudo, who as soon as he saw us refused to leave us, telling me that we must go through the territory of his king, where we would want for nothing; and so it proved from the time we met him until he led us to Inhambane.

[*D'Almada left what remained of the party at Inhambane, and went on to Sofala. From there he returned by ship with supplies and rescued them. Twenty-eight survivors finally reached Mozambique, more than a year after their landing.*]

35 / ATTEMPTED ASSASSINATION OF KING CHAKA OF THE ZULUS

In the first quarter of the nineteenth century, the notorious Chaka, warrior king of the Zulus, conquered and consolidated a powerful kingdom covering most of modern Natal. This description of an incident at his court was given by Henry Fynn, a member of an expedition which went to Zululand in 1824 to ascertain the source of the gold and ivory that reached the coast at Delagoa Bay. Thirteen days after leaving Port Natal, in July 1824, the expedition reached Umlatuzi, where Chaka's kraal was situated.

The whole country, so far as our sight could reach, was covered with numbers of people and droves of cattle. The king came up to us and told us not to be afraid of his people, who were coming onward. The cattle had been assorted according to their color, each drove being thus distinguished from others near it. A distinction

Henry Fynn, in *Annals of Natal*, by J. Bird. From *South African Explorers*, by Eric Axelson (Oxford, 1954), pp. 170-78.

[17] De Morais had died and d'Almada had been elected leader.

had also been made from the shape of the horns. These had been twisted by some art or skill into various forms, and to some additional horns had been attached—as many as four, six, or even eight—part of which were erect, part hung loosely down. There were instances of cattle on which strips of skin, cut from the hide but not detached from it, were hanging loosely from the bodies of the oxen. After exhibiting their cattle for two hours, they drew together in a circle, and sang and danced to the war whoop. Then the people returned to the cattle, again exhibiting them as before, and at intervals dancing and singing. The women now entered the kraal, each having a long thin stick in the right hand, and moving it in time to the song. They had not been dancing many minutes, when they had to make way for the ladies of the seraglio, besides about one hundred and fifty distinguished by the apellation of "sisters." These danced in parties of eight, each party wearing different colored beads, which were crossed from the shoulders to the knees. Each wore a headdress of black feathers, and four brass collars fitting close to the neck. The king joining in the dance was accompanied by the men. The dance lasted half an hour. The king then made a long speech.

On the following day he sent for me, and on my arrival asked me to look at a drove of cattle, which I had not yet seen, and to count them. I did so. There were 5,654. When I stated this result of my count, it caused very general laughter: and they asked how it was possible that I could count so many, since I had not once reckoned ten with my fingers. They came to the conclusion I had not counted at all, and the interpreter could not persuade Chaka of the possibility of counting without the use of the fingers. The Zulus have no other mode of reckoning. They commence from the little finger of the right hand, the thumb of the left hand representing six, and so in rotation to ten, which is the little finger of the left hand; twenty being two tens, thirty three tens, until they come to ten tens, or a hundred, which they call a "great" ten. There are some who have an idea of a thousand, which they call a "great" *ingwanu.* Chaka went on to speak of the gifts of nature. He said that the forefathers of the Europeans had bestowed on us many gifts, by giving us all the knowledge of arts and manufactures, yet they had kept from us the greatest of gifts, a good black skin: for this did not necessitate the wearing of clothes to hide the white skin, which was not pleasant to the eye. He well knew that for a black skin we would give all we were worth, our arts and manufactures.

The following day was spent in dancing, and this was kept up till evening. Having spent the afternoon in reading, I was induced to take another peep at the dancers. As it was dark when I came, the king ordered a number of people to hold up bundles of dried reeds, kept burning, to give light to the scene. I had not been there many minutes when I heard a shriek: and the lights were immediately extinguished. Then followed a general bustle and a cry. Having left Jacob (as I shall henceforth call the interpreter) and Michael, the Hottentot, at the hut, I endeavored to ask of every one who would give me a hearing what was the occasion of this extraordinary commotion. I found at length that Chaka, while dancing, had been stabbed. I immediately turned away to call Michael, whom I found at no great distance, shouting and giving the Hurrah, mistaking the confusion for some merriment. I immediately told him what I had heard, and sent him to prepare a lamp, and to bring some camomile, the only medicine I had by me. I also desired him to send the interpreter. The bustle and confusion was all this time very great. Jacob and Michael arriving, we proceeded to Chaka's hut in the palace, where we supposed him to be. Jacob, joining in the general uproar, fell down in a fit, so that now I could ask no questions or gain information as to where Chaka was. I attempted to gain admittance into his hut. There was a crowd round it. My lamp was put out. The women of the seraglio pulled me, some one way, some another; they were in a state of madness. The throng still increasing, and the uproar, with shrieks and cries, becoming dreadful, my situation was awkward and unpleasant in the extreme. Just as I was making another attempt to enter the hut, in which I supposed the king to be, a man, carrying some lighted reeds, attempted to drag me away, and on my refusal to accompany him . . . he made a second effort to pull me along, and was then assisted by another. I thought it best to see the result, and, if anything were intended against myself, to make the best of it. I walked with them for about five minutes, and my fears and suspicions were then relieved, for I saw the king in a kraal immediately near. I at once washed the wound with camomile tea and bound it up with linen. He had been stabbed with an assegai through the left arm, and the blade had passed through the ribs under the left breast. It must have been due to mere accident that the wound had not penetrated the lungs, but it made the king spit blood. His own doctor, who appeared to have a good knowledge in wounds, gave him a vomit, and afterward repeated doses of purging medicine, and continually washed the wound with decoctions of cooling roots. He also probed the wound to ascertain if any poison had been used on the assegai. Chaka cried nearly the whole night, expecting that only fatal consequences would ensue. The crowd had now increased so much that the noise of their shrieks was unbearable. Morning showed a horrid sight in clear light. I am satisfied that I cannot describe the scene in any words that would be of force to convey an impression to any reader sufficiently distinct of that hideous scene. Immense crowds of people were constantly arriving, and began their shouts when they came in sight of the kraal, running and exerting their utmost powers of voice as they entered it. They joined those already there, pulling one another about, throwing themselves down, without heeding how they fell, men and women indiscriminately. Many fainted from overexertion and excessive heat. The females of the seraglio more particularly were in very great distress, having overexerted themselves during the night, suffering from the stifling hot air, choked by the four brass collars fitting tight round their necks, so that they could not turn their heads, and faint from want of nourishment, which they did not dare to touch. Several of them died. Finding their situation so distressing, and there being no one to offer them relief, I procured a quantity of water and threw it over them as they fell, till I was myself so tired as to be obliged to desist. Then, however, they made some attempt to help each other. All this time I had been so busily employed as not to see the most sickening part of the tragical scene. They had begun to kill one another. Some were put to death because they did not weep, others for putting spittle in their eyes, others for sitting down to cry, although strength and tears, after such continuous exertion and mourning, were wholly exhausted. We then understood that six men had been wounded by the same assassins who wounded

Chaka. From the road they took it was supposed they had been sent by Zuedi, king of the Endwandwe, who was Chaka's only powerful enemy. Accordingly two regiments were sent at once in search of the aggressors.

I now washed his [Chaka's] wound frequently, and gave him mild purgatives. I dressed his wounds with ointment. The king, however, was hopeless for four days. During all that time people were flocking in from the outskirts of the country, joining in the general tumult. It was not till the fourth day that cattle were killed for the sustenance of the multitude. Many had died in the interval, and many had been killed for not mourning, or having gone to their kraals for food. On the fifth day there were symptoms of improvement in the king's health and wounds, and the favorable indications were even more noticeable on the day following. At noon, the party sent out in search of the malefactors returned, bringing with them the dead bodies of three men whom they had killed in the bush. These were the supposed murderers. The bodies were laid on the ground at a distance of about a mile from the kraal. The ears having been cut off from the right side of the heads, the two regiments sat down on either side of the road. Then all the people, men and women, probably exceeding 30,000, who had collected at the kraal, passed up the road, crying and screaming. Each one coming up to the bodies struck them several blows with a stick, which was then dropped on the spot: so that before half the number had come to the bodies, nothing more of them was to be seen; only an immense pile of sticks remained, but the formal ceremony still went on. The whole body now collecting, and three men walking in advance with sticks on which were the ears of the dead men, the procession moved up to Chaka's kraal. The king now made his appearance. The national mourning song was chanted; and, a fire being made in the center of the kraal, the ears were burned to ashes.

From the moment that Chaka had been stabbed, there had been a prohibition to wear ornaments, to wash the body, or to shave; and no man whose wife was pregnant had been allowed to come into the king's presence. All transgressions of these regulations being punishable with death, several human beings had been put to death.

There being now every appearance of Chaka's complete recovery, the chiefs and principal men brought cattle as an offering of thanksgiving; and on the next day the chief women did the same. Chaka then offered victims to the spirit of his deceased father.

FURTHER READINGS

For students wishing to explore further the African past, the best general works that are easily available are: Roland Oliver and J. D. Fage, *A Short History of Africa*; C. G. Seligman, *Races of Africa*; Basil Davidson, *The Lost Cities of Africa* and *Black Mother*.

Other anthologies to be recommended are: Basil Davidson, *The African Past*; M. Perham and J. Simmons, *African Discovery*; Thomas Hodgkin, *Nigerian Perspectives*; Freda Wolfson, *Pageant of Ghana*; C. Howard and J. H. Plumb, *West African Explorers*; Eric Axelson, *South African Explorers*.

Important works of exploration which have been recently reprinted are: Mary Kingsley, *Travels in West Africa* and *West African Studies*; Richard Burton, *The Lake Regions of Central Africa*. There are translations of Portuguese exploration available in Hakluyt Society publications: C. F. Beckingham and G. W. B. Huntingford, *The Prester John of The Indies;* C. R. Boxer, *The Tragic History of The Sea*. The sixteenth century account of the kingdom of Congo by Duarte Lopez and Filipo Pigafetta has been translated into French by Willi Bal as *Description du Royaume de Congo et des contrées environnantes*. J. Simmonds, *Livingstone and Africa* and Alan Morehead, *The White Nile* are useful books on the subject of African exploration.

Finally, the following regional historical works make good background reading: E. W. Bovill, *The Golden Trade of the Moors*; J. D. Fage, *Introduction to the History of West Africa;* Michael Crowder, *The Story of Nigeria;* Adu Boahen, *Britain, The Sahara, and The Western Sudan, 1788-1861;* A. H. M. Jones and E. Monroe, *A History of Ethiopia;* Roland Oliver and Gervase Mathew, *History of East Africa* (Vol. I); James Duffy, *Portuguese Africa*.